Illustrated

Tank & AFV

BUYER'S ★ GUIDE™

Michael Green

Motorbooks International
Publishers & Wholesalers ®

To my good friend Christopher F. Foss,
whose help and support have allowed me to
complete this book and many others.

First published in 1993 by Motorbooks
International Publishers & Wholesalers, PO Box 2,
729 Prospect Avenue, Osceola, WI 54020 USA

© Michael Green, 1993

Motorbooks International books are also available
at discounts in bulk quantity for industrial or sales-
promotional use. For details write to Special Sales
Manager at the Publisher's address

Library of Congress Cataloging-in-Publication
Data

Green, Michael.
    Illustrated tank & AFV buyer's guide /
    Michael Green.
        p.   cm. — (Motorbooks International
        illustrated buyer's guide series)
    Includes index.
    ISBN 0-87938-794-7
    1. Tanks (Military science)—Collectors and
    collecting. 2. Armored vehicles, Military—
    Collectors and collecting. I. Title. II. Title:
    Illustrated tank and AFV buyer's guide. III.
    Series.
    UG446.5.G688   1993
    358'.18'075—dc20   93–29850

On the front cover: Collector Jacques Littlefield
drives his immaculately restored Super Sherman.

On the back cover: Top, if you think it takes a
while to wash and detail your Corvette, wait till
you have to wash your Grizzly tank! Bottom,
armored cars are much more practical than tanks
for the collector of modest means. Shown here is
a Dingo, built for the British Army during World
War II. *Bill Nahmens*

Printed and bound in the United States of America

Contents

Acknowledgments

Special thanks for help in putting this book together go to Richard A. Pemberton, Dick Hunnicutt, Richard Bryd, Fred Ropkey, Skip Warvel, Fred Pernell, Dennis R. Spence, William F. Atwater, Kenneth Powers, Jim Mesko, Michael O'Brien, William U. Rosenmund, George Bradford, Roy Hamilton, Bill Nahmens, David Fletcher, George Forty, John Upton, Sloane Upton, Randy Kricke, Thomas O. Berndt, Dennis M. Riva, David Marian, and Jacques M. Littlefield.

Organizations that kindly extended their help were *AFV News*; *Armor* magazine; The Patton Museum, Fort Knox, Kentucky; The Ordnance Museum at Aberdeen Proving Ground, Maryland; and the National Archives, Washington, DC.

Introduction

One of the fastest-growing fields of interest in the vintage or specialized vehicle category is the collecting of military vehicles (MV). While most MV collectors own unarmored wheeled vehicles such as the WWII-era jeep, other historical MVs, such as half-tracks, armored cars, and tanks, are becoming increasingly popular. Thanks to war movies and television, all of these vehicles are probably familiar to most people, but the average person would be amazed to hear that somebody could even own an armored fighting vehicle (AFV). Yet, this same person might have recently attended any one of the hundreds of air shows that are held throughout the country on a regular basis. The aircraft featured at these shows are owned by individuals. It's easy to understand why someone would want to collect former-military aircraft, especially those of WWII fame such as the P-51 Mustang and the B-17 Flying Fortress. But AFVs do not have the same sleek functional lines of airplanes or any of the romantic spirit of adventure found with planes—making it much harder for the public to understand why anybody would want to own a tank.

However, like the owners of historical military aircraft, AFV collectors think that their vehicles should be preserved as valuable relics for future generations to study and enjoy. A small number of museums in both the United States and overseas specialize in preserving AFVs, but they are all plagued by limited funding and shortages of personnel to restore the vehicles. If it were not for the dedication of a few individual collectors, many historical military vehicles would have disappeared.

The AFVs that are in the hands of private collectors are, like their military aircraft counterparts, no longer functional weapons systems. Their machine guns and cannons were long ago rendered inoperable by the welder's torch (dummy guns are available now). The hulls of many AFVs were cut into pieces and sold for scrap metal, and only with the tender loving care and skills of collectors have these vehicles been restored.

This book will attempt to portray in very broad terms and photos the thrill of collecting AFVs. It will characterize the types of collectors and some of the vehicles they collect (there are hundreds of different types), and for those whose interest begins to grow, it tells where these vehicles can be found and how much they may cost.

Chapter 1

The Collectors

Fred Ropkey, an Indianapolis, Indiana, businessman who owns the largest collection of AFVs in the United States, traces his interest in acquiring AFVs back to age eight, when his father gave him a Revolutionary War sword, sparking a lifelong interest in a variety of military artifacts.

In 1946, a year after WWII ended, Ropkey paid $150 for his first AFV, an M3A1 American-built scout car. After restoring this war-weary vehicle to mint condition, Ropkey began thinking about buying and fixing up other WWII survivors. Unfortunately, Ropkey's new career in the US Marine Corps (USMC) put the brakes on this. But fate works in strange ways, and during the Korean War, Ropkey found himself a lieutenant in charge of a platoon of WWII-era Sherman tanks.

His war-time experience behind him, Ropkey returned home with renewed interest to start collecting AFVs. Ropkey decided that helping him restore old AFVs would be a good way to keep his two growing boys out of youthful trouble, and with their help, by the 1970s, his tank collection shifted into high gear. Today, Ropkey has more than 100 MVs of varying types, including forty AFVs ranging from American Sherman tanks to Russian armored cars.

Ropkey has on occasion lent his vehicles to both Hollywood and television companies. The money earned by these activities aids in defraying the sometimes very expensive costs of restoring the vehicles themselves.

His favorite tank, an early-war M4A3 Sherman medium tank named *Liberty*, had a co-starring role with actor James Garner in the appropriately named movie *Tank*. In 1983, the movie company rented two of Ropkey's Sherman tanks, the second being a backup in case the first broke down. After hauling the two tanks to Georgia, where the movie was filmed, Ropkey and an employee, Skip Warvel, taught James Garner and a couple of other actors how to drive them.

According to Warvel, the tanks performed very well, destroying cars, trees, and a $100,000 building on cue. Warvel and Ropkey's biggest worry was that the tanks might break down at a critical moment of filming and stop a multimillion dollar film production. Fortunately, the tanks performed like true stars and never failed.

The Garner movie was the third film role for Ropkey's tanks. Earlier film roles included *The Blue Brothers* starring Dan Aykroyd and the late John Belushi. In *The Blues Brothers*, Ropkey personally drove one of his AFVs through the heart of downtown Chicago into Daley Plaza. According to Ropkey, it was one of the most interesting experiences a tank collector could have.

Ropkey's tanks have also appeared in a made-for-television movie called *Special Bulletin*, in which a large southern city is nuked by terrorists.

Jacques Littlefield, a California investor who owns one of the top five largest private

MV collections in the United States, remembers as a small child being interested in all types of mechanical gadgets, ranging from trains to construction equipment. As Littlefield grew older and could afford to spend money on collecting items of interest, everything from sports cars to pipe organs began to fill his garage. By age 40, Littlefield's collecting interest turned to military vehicles, particularly AFVs. Asked to explain his fascination with tanks, Littlefield responded: "I think they're more interesting than cars or trucks. They have a number of different subsystems like hydraulics, radios, turrets, guns, opticals, etc. I like their complexity and the fact that they're big. They are also very unusual to

own. I'm less interested in something that everybody's doing. I would rather do something that's a bit more unique."

Littlefield's first military vehicle was a WWII-era M3A1 scout car that he bought from an equipment supply company in 1975 for approximately $3,500. Littlefield quickly went to work restoring the vehicle to the same standard as when it rolled off the factory floor in 1944. With his newly developed interest, Littlefield set about acquiring additional AFVs.

More typical of AFV collectors is Roy Hamilton, who owns only a handful of vehicles. Hamilton describes how he got started in the hobby: "When I was about eleven years

Wearing a WWII American tanker's helmet, a very young Fred Ropkey sits in his first AFV, a WWII-era American M3A1 scout car. *Fred Ropkey*

old, I became interested in collecting military artifacts. Having also acquired an interest in fixing cars, I later became an auto mechanic. In 1974, a friend of mine gave me a 1944 Dodge three-quarter-ton military commander car. The vehicle was in pretty sad shape. Since I had a Volkswagen repair shop at that time, I decided to go ahead and rebuild the vehicle. Having never attempted this type of project before, I spent a great deal of time studying the subject of military vehicles before starting the restoration of the command car. With my twin interest in both mechanical and military artifacts, I became more involved in collecting other military vehicles. As time went on, I acquired at least three M20 armored cars, two of which I have already restored. Yet, my biggest desire was to find a small tank that I could rebuild. I was very fortunate in 1983, when I managed to buy an M5A1 light tank from a surplus equipment dealer. I've been collecting replacement parts for this vehicle for years, but due to my funding limits, I've been unable to complete this project as of yet. I may, in the future, sell one of my remaining M20 armored cars and use the money to finish my tank."

Relative newcomers to the field of AFV collecting are brothers John and Sloane Upton, proud owners of a recently restored former-

Army M39 armored utility vehicle. The Uptons trace their interests in acquiring an AFV back to their youths. As young boys, they were often told stories by their father (who served in World War I) about the first British tanks to see combat. During WWII, the Upton family home became a mecca for many British officers since the Upton family was very involved in the local British relief fund. Many a wartime story was told to the Upton brothers by the men visiting their home. It was from these stories that the two brothers developed a lifelong interest in many aspects of WWII technology. The M39 now owned by them was based on a WWII-era American-built tank destroyer known as the M18 Hellcat.

Armed with a 76mm gun, the M18 first saw combat in Italy in early 1944. Approximately 2,500 M18s were built between June 1943 and October 1943. Of these 2,500 vehicles, the first 640 were later returned to the factory and converted into M39 armored utility vehicles. The M18 and M39 were both powered by an aircraft-type radial gas engine and remain the fastest AFVs ever placed into production. An M18 was clocked at Aberdeen Proving Ground, Maryland, with a top speed of 62mph. Most M39s were used by the Army during late WWII as gun-towing vehicles. After WWII, they were converted into ar-

After becoming a successful businessman, Fred Ropkey had the funds to acquire additional AFVs. He is pictured here (on the right) conferring with a friend on the rewiring of a WWII-era American-built half-track. *Fred Ropkey*

As time went on, Fred Ropkey's collection grew in size. Pictured is a small part of his collection during the early 1980s. The two vehicles in the foreground are both WWII-era M4A3 Sherman tanks, followed by a Sherman tank-based armored recovery vehicle. Other vehicles include an M5 light tank and a 40mm towed antiaircraft gun at the far end. *Fred Ropkey*

mored personnel carriers (APCs) and saw heavy use during the Korean War. The last M39 was phased out of US service in early 1957.

To date, the Upton M39 is the only vehicle of its class that the Uptons have completely restored to operational condition. Being very fortunate in owning an 83-acre vineyard in northern California, the Uptons have a variety of gravel trails on which to operate this very unique AFV.

Restoring any large mechanical gadget, from truck to farm tractor, can be both difficult and time-consuming. Bill Nahmens, an AFV mechanic who doesn't own any of his own MVs but works on the collections of oth-

ers, describes the effort involved in rebuilding a tank: "I would say the most difficult part is the weight of the components. Everything is done with a crane. A person could get by if he had a little front-end loader, or even a small forklift would be ideal, because the components are too heavy for one person to lift. Some of the components can be lifted by two people, but to hold them in position and get them fastened to the vehicle, you need something that's stationary. I think one of the hardest restoration decisions is [to resist the temptation] to take shortcuts. It's real easy to tell yourself, 'Well, nobody's going to see this way down under the engine since all the wiring's enclosed in conduits. So, let's just go

Posed in front of his favorite tank, an M4A3 Sherman nicknamed *Liberty*, Fred Ropkey was at the time preparing to ship *Liberty* and a backup tank to be used in the Hollywood movie *Tank*. *Fred Ropkey*

Like most military vehicle collectors, Fred Ropkey has always been very happy to share his interest in military vehicles. In addition to appearing in television shows and movies, Fred's vehicles have been seen in numerous parades throughout the Midwest. Pictured in a Fourth of July parade in Indianapolis, Indiana, is one of his Sherman tanks, followed by an M19 antiaircraft vehicle and an M3A1 half-track. *Fred Ropkey*

To help defray the expense of restoring older military vehicles, many collectors rent their vehicles for either television or movie work. Pictured is one of Fred Ropkey's Sherman tanks taking part in a television commercial for a local company. *Fred Ropkey*

down to the neighborhood Kragen's Auto Parts and buy the plastic wiring.' But here, we go with the cloth wiring, the original cloth wiring and the correct color code on the cloth wiring. We want to stay original and quite detailed, probably more detailed than it would be out of the factory."

Because most people who want to collect AFVs don't have the room to store or maintain them properly, smaller tanks are much more popular and valuable than bigger and heavier tanks. Smaller tanks under 20 tons can be moved with tilt-bed trailers or dump trucks or other civilian construction equipment, and they can be stored in a slightly enlarged regular garage.

For those collectors who can afford to buy an AFV but don't have the space, time, tools, or skills to restore them, a number of individuals have set themselves up in the business of restoring and preserving historical military vehicles. Depending on your needs and funds, these talented people can restore a military vehicle from the ground up if necessary. Also, with the growing popularity of restoring AFVs, a number of small cottage industries have begun to reproduce a wide variety of hard-to-find components, ranging from

armor plates to ammunition racks that are currently unobtainable to collectors.

While most collectors of AFVs must make do with dummy machine guns and cannons that have been demilitarized by the welder's torch, a very small number of collectors have secured federal firearms permits for operational cannons. Collectors must, however, reload their own ammunition. Since most collectors do not have the skills to do this, very few have had the opportunity to actually fire their tank cannons.

The best possible combination of elements for a tank or AFV collector is to own a shop or business that has an overhead crane or a pull-around crane. For those collectors not so lucky, Jacques Littlefield describes what is needed to restore a tank or other large AFV: "You need an area where there is sufficient room to gain access to all sides of the vehicle for workers as well as lifting equipment, and additional space (probably at least two to three times the space occupied by the vehicle) to store the parts as they are removed and rebuilt; naturally, a covered area is best , but excellent restorations have been done under tarps and temporary roofs. Electricity for lights, welders, and air compressors is a must. Heating, cooling fans, and ventilation requirements will depend on the local weather, but the hobby is much more pleasant when these are taken into account.

"The basic process involves disassembling the vehicle (a camera for pictures is a must if you want to be able to reassemble it properly); sandblasting the old paint and rust; brazing, welding, and filling the old parts; degreasing and painting them; and reassembly. A variety of different welders, paint guns, electric, air, and hand tools will be used, typically of larger scale than in the average auto shop. A drill press (at least 12in capacity), powered grinders, a band saw, variable-speed drills, 1/2 and 3/4in impact wrenches and sockets, and portable hydraulic rams are a sample of what will be required.

"A gas torch will be necessary to loosen larger rusted nuts and bolts, a hydraulic press will be needed to assemble bearings and seals, and a variety of electric and auto test equipment will be necessary to time the engines and troubleshoot the wiring.

"It is always nice to have engine lathes, milling machines, a hydraulic ironworker, a metal-cutting band saw, an arbor press, and sheet metal equipment for making parts, but in many cases these are used infrequently and the work can best be done at a local business or school.

"It will be necessary to have a safe way of handling heavy parts while they are removed, processed, and reassembled. People use everything from overhead cranes to roll-around cranes, Gantry (A-frame) cranes, forklifts, front-end loaders, or military wrecking cranes. Some heavier-capacity bottle and floor jacks will be needed as well. Remember, most of these vehicles are designed to be maintained easily, but only if the proper tools are used. Skimping on the quality of the tools or overstressing their capacity will result in frustration, skinned knuckles, or possibly a more severe injury.

When buying a used tank, a "fixer-upper" is normally what you get. Pictured is an M41 American-built light tank that saw its last role as a range target. Collectors typically buy one or two models of the same vehicle, hoping that will give them enough parts to restore at least one to operational condition. *Michael Green*

"Last but not least, it helps to have the appropriate manuals, most of which are available from various sources within the hobby, as well as other books with photos of the vehicle. Patience and the realization that all these processes take more time than for other typical hobbies will help put things into perspective and add to a feeling of satisfaction at the end of the job. Placing the rear end of a half-track next to the rear end of a Ford Mustang will give you some idea of what the scale of things is. If that does not impress you, take a look at the front axle of an M26 Pershing or the steering unit of a Sherman Tank."

Where Do You Find AFVs?

Of the hundreds of thousands of AFVs built and placed into use since World War I, very few have survived long enough to pass into the hands of private collectors. Most AFVs built in the United States and considered obsolete by the American military are either scrapped and then sold or given under military assistance programs to friendly governments. Others find their way to military firing ranges.

The only exception to this rule occurs when the federal government allows the military to retain certain AFVs for their historical value. Such vehicles are often on display at military bases within the United States and overseas. The government will also loan these vehicles to private, nonprofit museums for display. There are very strict rules: The government will allow the vehicles to be restored, if needed, but the government retains the right to reclaim the vehicles.

Various AFVs have also been donated, as monuments, to veterans' groups. These vehicles can be seen across the United States in both small towns and cities.

In contrast, the American public has been barred by the federal government from buying surplus AFVs since the mid-1950s.

Most of the AFVs now in private hands date from the period between the end of WWII (1945) and the mid-1950s. At that time, heavy equipment and scrap dealers bought numerous leftover WWII American half-tracks and tanks. The heavy equipment dealers had visions of converting the AFVs into use by agricultural and construction interests, and the US and Canadian lumber industry converted many WWII-era half-tracks to log haulers. But most AFVs, especially tanks, are so specialized for their wartime missions that there is almost no comparable civilian job for them. There is a story of an enterprising gentleman in the late 1940s who bought a surplus M4 Sherman tank for demolition work. Unfortunately, while trying to knock down a house with his tank, the heavy weight of the vehicle collapsed the ground floor of the building he was in. The tank fell into the building's basement and everything else fell or collapsed on top of it. The owner of the demolition tank suffocated to death. Another story is of a midwestern farmer who thought that a surplus Sherman tank might make a good, inexpensive farm tractor. As he drove

The typical fate of most obsolete AFVs, like this rare late-war Japanese Army tank, is to be used as range targets. This before-and-after picture shows to good effect the results of a high-velocity tank round. *Fred Ropkey*

One of the most expensive parts of buying AFVs is the shipping costs. Tanks and other AFVs tend to be both large and heavy. To ship these items by boat, train, or truck can sometimes double their purchase costs. Some collectors get around this problem by buying their own trucks. This beautiful Kenworth is owned by Jacques Littlefield, who uses it to transport some of his military vehicles. *Michael Green*

over a local bridge, the heavy vehicle fell through the bottom of the bridge's roadbed, killing the farmer and destroying the tank.

For many American and European scrap dealers who bought AFVs after WWII, with plans to torch them for their scrap metal value, the time-consuming job of trying to cut up tanks proved unprofitable. Because of this, many of these same vehicles survived for years in the far reaches of scrap yards to be later discovered and bought by collectors. Those vehicles converted into civilian roles in the logging, construction, or farming business, were eventually left to rot in some field or company storage facility as newer, specially designed vehicles appeared on the market.

A few AFVs were passed from the US military to federal and state agencies or local governments. They were used as everything from large snowplows to police riot-control vehi-cles. As time went on, these former-military vehicles were also left to gather dust as they broke down or wore out. It was up to collectors to find them and restore them.

According to Tom Berndt, unofficial historian for the MV hobby, collecting AFVs began in earnest in the United States in the early 1970s. "Armor was rare before that time in collectors' hands. A number of MV collectors who already owned wheeled military vehicles like jeeps or trucks just decided to make the jump into armor. At first, the AFVs most often collected were the WWII-era American-made half-tracks. This was because so many had survived after the war into civilian roles. There were also a number of companies who still had lots of parts for the vehicles. After awhile, collectors got bored with the half-tracks and began looking for armored cars like the American-made WWII-era M8 and

Collectors need heavy-duty overhead cranes to re-store larger and heavier AFVs such as main battle tanks. Pictured at the home of Jacques Littlefield in his specially built tank garage is the turret of an M26 Pershing medium tank being removed from its hull. *Michael Green*

M20 armored cars. These vehicles were much harder to find and commanded very high prices for awhile. When interest leveled off in these vehicles, collectors' interest turned to American-made WWII light tanks like the M3 and M5."

As the economic boom times of the 1980s began, collectors who had the money to spend began looking for AFVs to buy. In 1981, the Portuguese Army sold to a heavy equipment supply Co. in Georgia a large number of former-American and Canadian-built tanks and self-propelled artillery guns. Included in this sale were at least seventy American-built WWII M5A1 light tanks.

Roughly half of these vehicles were quickly bought up by collectors. The remaining vehicles took an additional six years to be sold off.

With this dramatic surge of interest, a number of full-time and part-time dealers in the United States and overseas set up shop to fulfill collectors' desires. These same dealers then began to search around the world for AFVs that could be bought and then sold to collectors for a profit. As a result, many WWII-era AFVs passed on to Third World nations over the years returned to the countries where they were built.

This was in complete contrast to the 1960s when another heavy equipment supply Co. in Tennessee had managed to buy more than 100 surplus WWII-era American M3 light tanks but couldn't find anybody to buy them. All of the M3s were cut up for scrap metal.

Three major publications devoted to the MV hobby feature a large number of ads for AFVs. While there are numerous other publications that may feature an occasional ad for the sale of an AFV, these offer the greatest variety of vehicles for sale:

Military Vehicles (The Marketplace for Military Vehicles): Published six times a year by Eagle Press, P.O. Box 1748, Union, N.J. 07083. Subscription rates are $15 a year in the United States and $24 a year in Canada.

Supply Line: Published six times a year by the Military Vehicle Preservation Association, P.O. Box 520378, Independence, MO. Membership in the association costs $30 a year in the United States and includes *Supply Line*.

Wheels and Tracks (The International Review of Military Vehicles): Published four times a year by Battle of Britain Prints International Ltd., Church House, London E15 3JA, England. The US trade distributor in charge of subscriptions is Bill Dean Books Ltd., P.O. Box 69, Whitestone, NY 11357.

For those interested in generalized AFV history, an excellent source of information is the *AFV News* newsletter, published by the

Bill Nahmens, an AFV restorer, is using an overhead crane to lift the stripped-down hull of an Army M5A1 light tank from the shop floor. Built during WWII, the M5A1 light tank was armed only with a puny 37mm cannon. *Michael Green*

Armored Fighting Vehicle Association. The newsletter comes out three times a year and is available at an annual worldwide subscription rate of $14. The newsletter and membership in the association are available from George Bradford, editor of *AFV News*, at R.R. 32, Cambridge, Ontario, Canada N3H 4R7. Another good source of AFV information is *Armor* magazine, a professional trade journal for American military tank men published bimonthly by the Army Armor Center, at Fort Knox, Kentucky. Within its pages you will find a good cross-section of articles ranging from historical to how to train an M1A1 Abrams tank crewman in his job. Top experts in the field also contribute outstanding articles about foreign AFVs and tactics. Subscription information is available from the US Armor Association at P.O. Box 607, Fort Knox, Kentucky 40121.

Portrayal Press, owned by Dennis R. Spence, is a mail order book Co. that specializes in publications on military vehicles of all types. In addition to books and magazines, Dennis offers an extensive selection of US military manuals for everything from jeeps to tanks. These manuals are an absolute necessity for any AFV collector who wishes to own and operate any type of American-made military vehicle. A catalog is available from Portrayal Press at P.O. Box 1190, Andover, New Jersey 07821.

Before you can repaint an older AFV, you sometimes need to sandblast off the rust and old paint. Using a truck-mounted crane, a makeshift sandblasting setup is created here. The vehicle being sandblasted is a hull from an Army M5A1 light tank. *Michael Green*

Forklifts are very important to collectors of heavier AFVs since the component parts of these vehicles tend to be both large and heavy. This forklift is being used to remove one of the two engines that powered an Army M24 light tank. *Michael Green*

If you are interested in videotapes on military vehicles, John Seburn owns a mail order firm named "Vintage Video" that features rare military training films, factory films, film bulletins from WWII, and a number of other special interest films. Catalogues are available from Vintage Video, P.O. Box 551, Greencastle, Pennsylvania 17225.

Selling Terms

HULK: This is a vehicle that is largely intact with many missing pieces, such as the tires, tracks, or engines, readily available elsewhere, but due to exposure, rust, and so on,

quite a bit of work will be required to get everything operational. A vehicle that was in a city park for forty years, for example, would be a typical hulk.

OPERATIONAL: This is a vehicle that is basically complete, with a reasonable paint job (not sandblasted to bare metal, but repainted after sanding), and is still operational and looking as it did at the end of its useful life in the military. Depending on the level of completeness, this vehicle might have been fitted with demilitarized armament, but will probably lack such extras as radios, optics, and markings. Most AFVs offered for sale in the hobby would fall into this category.

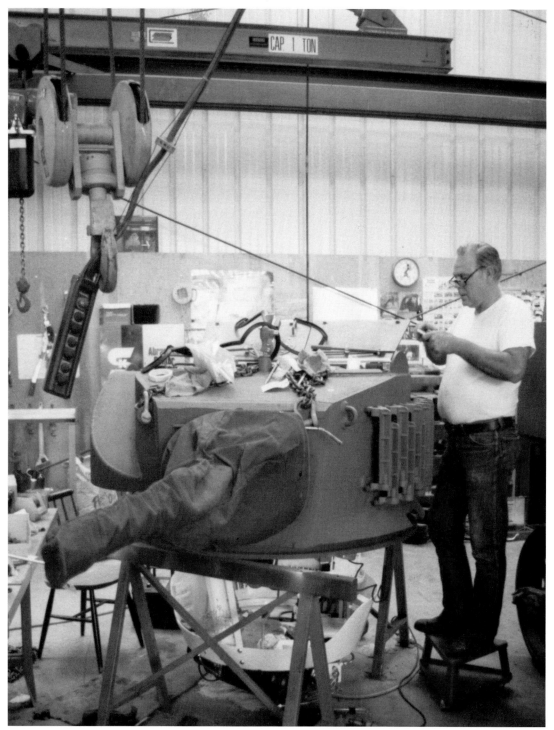

Roy Hamilton, military vehicle buff and restorer, is
working on the final details of the turret of an Army
M5A1 light tank. *Michael Green*

RESTORED: This is a vehicle that has been totally disassembled and all parts cleaned, plated, painted, per the original specifications. The engine, transmission, rear end, steering unit, and tires (or tracks) will be rebuilt to like-new standards and will be fully operational. All other subsystems (fire extinguishers, ventilation, storage boxes, decals, weapons mounts, seats, stabilizers, and so on) will be complete and operational. The final result should represent a vehicle just delivered from the factory and equipped by the Army unit or depot so that it would be ready to go into battle with the addition of live ammunition, rations, fuel, and a crew. This level of restoration is seen in a number of "soft-skinned" military vehicles, such as jeeps and command cars, and occasionally in half-tracks, scout cars, and armored cars, such as the M8 and M20, but today is quite rare. In this configuration, the vehicles are considered museum pieces and are not to be driven.

Some older-generation AFVs considered obsolete and not destroyed on firing ranges are kept for their historical value by military museums. This Army M103 heavy tank, armed with a very long, 120mm cannon, is on permanent display at Fort Hood, Texas. *Bill Rosenmund*

Cleaning tanks is no fun, but it is a necessary job. Pictured is a Canadian-built copy of the American M4A1 Sherman tank, known as the Grizzly. The Canadians built 188 Grizzlies before production was halted. Many of these vehicles were given to Portugal and were later sold to a British dealer. *Michael Green*

Chapter 2

The Beginnings of the Tank

During World War I (1914-1918), machine guns, artillery, barbed wire, and field fortifications gave the defense a distinct advantage that neither side's offense could overcome by

The first tanks to see combat in World War I had a very odd, rhomboidal shape with overhead tracks. This was designed to help them cross the many wide trenches that dotted the landscape of Western Europe. Being about 8ft tall, 32ft long, and 13ft 9in wide, the early British tanks had a crew of eight men. Using gas engines of about 200hp, the vehicles had a top speed of about 4mph and an operational range of fewer than 25 miles. *Michael Green*

numerical superiority. Initially, each tried to break the stalemate by preceding infantry assaults with longer and more intense artillery bombardments. The concept was that artillery would first "take" the ground. The infantry would then advance, mop up, and hold the ground. This method proved futile. While the ill-fated offensives caused millions of casualties, front lines did not change significantly for three years.

This stalemate caused the Allies (France and England) to look for some form of new technology to win the war. It was an English officer named Ernest Swinton who first visualized the concept of what would later become the tank.

Walking behind the lines one day, Swinton happened to see a small American-made Holt caterpillar tractor pushing itself through the mud and slush. Other vehicles were stopped cold. The little tractor seemed, on the other hand, unstoppable. An idea was thus born in Swinton's mind: Why couldn't these tractors be protected with enough armor to stop machine gun bullets? So equipped, these tractors could be sent across the no-man's-land that separated the warring sides and be used to crush and destroy the barbed wire and machine gun positions that had stopped the infantry on so many occasions.

Swinton returned to England in late 1914 to present his new idea to the top Allied military leaders—but there was little or no enthusiasm for the concept. The only person to see a future for this idea was Winston Churchill,

The first British tanks proved to be too slow and too heavy to effectively pursue a retreating enemy. The British Army decided it wanted a lighter, faster vehicle to take over the role once performed by cavalry units on horseback. The result was the Whippet medium tank, of which 200 were made during 1917–1918 for the British Army. Having a crew of three, the Whippet was armed with four machine guns and had a top speed of 8mph and an operational range of 40 miles. *National Archives*

then the First Lord of the Admiralty (British Navy). Long after the British Army had shelved the idea of armored tractors, Churchill continued to pursue the idea and organized his own group to carry on with experiments. The leader of Churchill's group was a naval ship designer. Because of the original British Naval influence on tank design, tankers from World War I until today refer to the various components of their vehicles with such nautical terms as the hull, the superstructure, the deck, the bow, the hatches, and the ports.

As time went on, the British Army became more interested in what the British Navy was doing with armored tractors, and eventually, the Army and Navy got together to pursue the development of armored tractors. While Churchill later left his position as the First Lord of the Admiralty, his belief in Swinton's idea had kept the ball rolling at a crucial time.

Why Are They Called Tanks?

As the British continued their work on armored tractors, they did their best to keep their experiments a complete secret from the Germans lest they find out early enough to develop countermeasures. The workmen putting the first armored tractors together did not know what they were building. They had been told that these vehicles were being built to carry large containers of water for use by British forces stationed in Egypt. Every written record related to the building of these vehicles was made under the heading of "water carriers." The workmen making these strange new vehicles decided for the sake of brevity to adopt the word "tank" as a nickname. The nickname stuck and is almost universally used to identify the vehicle.

Tanks were first used in Somme, France, in September 1916. Of the forty-nine tanks used, fifteen did not reach the assembly area and only eighteen entered the fight. Aside from mechanical problems, the tanks had difficulty maneuvering on the cratered and muddy battlefields. Additionally, they were committed piecemeal and were not coordinated with the infantry. The attack achieved some minor local successes but was not a major victory. However, the Allied commanders became quickly aware of the shock value that had been added to the assault on the German defensive positions. The French soon developed a number of their own tanks, while the Germans were forced to use captured British tanks, until they could develop a small number of their own during the later stages of the war. By the end of the war, tanks had been used in ninety-one combat engagements.

Early Evolution of the Tank

After World War I, most military thinkers saw the tank as a significant technological development but could not agree on the tactical doctrine for its deployment. More conservative military men believed future wars would

The French Army followed the British Army's lead in World War I and started to field its own tanks. Pictured is the Saint Chamond assault tank. Using the American-built Holt tractor as a basic chassis, the French added a large armored box. Armed with a fixed, forward-firing 75mm gun and at least four machine guns, the Saint Chamond assault tank had an impressive amount of firepower for its day. Unfortunately, its design layout was very awkward and not successful. About 400 were built for the French Army during World War I. *National Archives*

be relatively static, as in World War I. Hence, they saw the tank's role as providing mobile fire support for the infantry. This became known as the "infantry-support tank" doctrine.

Another group maintained that tanks should be used together, taking full advantage of their mobility. The Germans were the first to use this concept in battle when they invaded Poland in late September 1939 and, later, France in May 1940. The Germans had formed armored and motorized combine arms teams built around tanks (known as *panzers*) and armored infantry (or *panzer-grenadier*) riding in half-tracks, supported and assisted by armored scout cars, self-propelled artillery, and antitank guns, and backed up by air defense units. These ground units would work with close support aircraft such as the famous Stuka dive bomber.

The superiority of the mobile warfare doctrine over the infantry-support tank and its associated fixed-defense doctrine was dramatically demonstrated in France in the early days of WWII. In terms of both men and equipment, French and British forces had a combined strength that was greater than the Germans', but they chose to cling to fixed defenses with infantry-support tank units as a mobile reserve.

The German combined-arms teams, built around *panzer* and *panzer-grenadier* units, used the mobile warfare doctrine to achieve spectacular gains. From late summer of 1939 to the fall of 1941, the Germans did not suffer a serious defeat on land.

In response to the German mobile warfare doctrine of early WWII, the Americans, British, and Russians were forced to change their ways of thinking about tanks. Tanks

Also based on the American-designed Holt tractor chassis was the Schneider assault tank. This French Army tank was armed with a short-barreled 75mm gun mounted in the right side of the vehicle's superstructure. It had a crew of six and was powered by a gas engine. About 400 were built between 1917 and 1918. *National Archives*

The only World War I-era tank that survived into WWII was the French-designed Renault FT-17 light tank. First built in 1917, this two-man tank could be armed with either a machine gun or small, short-barreled 37mm cannon. Widely exported around the world after World War I, the Army had almost 1,000 slightly improved copies of the Renault light tank made between 1918 and 1919. In American service, the vehicle was known as the Six-Ton M1917 light tank. *National Archives*

would no longer be used as infantry support weapons only. They would themselves become a major combat arm. Deployed in mass, the Allied armies in WWII used the tank in combined-arms teams against the same German Army that had pioneered it. By 1943, the high water mark of German offensive action, the combined production capacity of the Allies began to overwhelm the German military machine. On the defensive, beginning in 1944, the German armored formations were slowly bled to death in a useless effort to stem the inevitable Allied victory over Nazi Germany.

Before the outbreak of WWII, tanks had generally evolved into light machine-gun-armed exploitation vehicles and heavier, slower assault tanks armed with a variety of machine guns and small cannons. As the war went on, the various warring sides became locked into a technological race to build tanks with bigger guns and heavier armor. At the

Military conflicts tend to dramatically speed up the weapons technology race. By the end of WWII, the Germans had developed tank destroyers like the 70-ton Jagdtiger armed with a 128mm high-velocity cannon and protected by steel armor up to 12in thick. *Michael Green*

A column of German light tanks advance into Poland in September 1939. The German use of combined-arms teams overwhelmed Polish static defenses. *Armor magazine*

start of WWII (1939), the typical tank had a cannon no bigger than 37mm and weighed about 12 tons. By the end of WWII (1945), some tanks had guns as large as 122mm and weighed up to 70 tons. It was these late war heavy tanks, like the famous German Tiger, that still form part of the popular image of what an AFV is.

The Cold War and Beyond

Essentially then, a modern tank is an armored, track-laying vehicle, armed with machine guns and a large-caliber, direct-fire cannon. It is characterized by its ability to bring a large volume of fire into a battlefield.

As the Cold War developed, the NATO armies continued to develop and improve the WWII-era tanks with more-powerful weapons and engines and heavier armor. Un-

fortunately, these developments have made the modern tank a very expensive and complex vehicle. The well-known American M1 and M1A1 Abrams tanks used to great effect during Operation Desert Storm costs approximately $3 million each. In contrast, the famous American Sherman tank of WWII cost $60,000 in its day.

The Soviets built up the greatest fleet of tanks in the world (50,000) during the post-war years. Unlike the United States and its NATO Allies, the Soviets generally concentrated on building large numbers of simpler, less complex, cheaper tanks designed to overwhelm the other side's armies.

Both sides of the now-ended Cold War designed their tanks with three main objectives in mind: firepower, armor protection, and mobility. The crux of the tank designers' problems was to design a tank with the prop-

Prior to the outbreak of WWII in late 1939, the US Army had fewer than 200 modern tanks, most of which were light tanks such as this M2A2, which had twin, one-man turrets fitted with machine guns only. This particular vehicle, belonging to the 193rd Tank Battalion (light) in August 1941, does not have its weapons mounted. *US Army*

American tanks such as the M4 Sherman series from WWII were seriously outgunned and underarmored compared to later-war German tanks. This uneven struggle can be seen in this German Army photo of two knocked-out M4 Shermans that have lost their turrets in combat. *Erling J. Foss*

er balance, as the parts of a tank are interdependent but opposed. Since both armor and large-caliber guns are heavy, mobility is sacrificed. A very fast and maneuverable tank must have a high horsepower-per-ton ratio and should be relatively small and light. To get more firepower and more armor protection, weight must be added—with a consequent loss in speed and maneuverability. Thus, a tank must be fitted to the mission it will perform. Between the 1950s and the 1960s, the Western Allies and the Soviets developed a number of different tanks to get a proper balance in capabilities. There were light, medium, and heavy tanks. By the early 1970s, the heavy tanks disappeared from most armies as the medium tank became able to carry cannons that once could only be carried by a heavy tank.

The tank's biggest problem has always been to stay one step ahead of the weapons designed to destroy it. While the public has always believed that tanks are like land battleships, dashing rapidly and invincibly around battlefields, blowing up everything in their paths, reality is just the opposite. Tanks are really very large, fragile, unreliable vehicles that are very vulnerable to an entire host of anti-

tank weapons, ranging from mines to missiles. Even the most modern main battle tanks, such as the American Abrams or the Soviet T72 or T80, have to be carried to their battlefield positions on enormous tank-transporter trucks.

On the battlefield, tanks have to be very careful where they travel. Like a barefoot kid in a cow pasture, they have to stay away from numerous features that they could get stuck in. Sand, loose gravel, mud, snow, rocks, trees, small streams, and riverbanks can all stop a tank cold.

Tanks are also very dangerous to their crews and all those around them. Even the most modern tanks are deaf, comparatively blind, and very uncomfortable to be in for even short periods of time. An excellent description of what it is like in a tank was described in a 1942 book entitled *Mechanized Might* by Maj. Paul C. Raborg published by Whittlesey House, a division of the McGraw-Hill Book Co., Inc.: "There are two gentle sports in the armies of today. One is indulged in by the parachute troops; the other, by the crews of tanks. There is much curiosity as to just what a tank ride is like. Such a trip over rough country at high speed is really so terrific and appalling that it begs description. By comparison, a bucking bronco is tame, a stunting airplane is mild. Find a nice level lawn, well studded with trees 6 or 8in in diameter. Now, get in your car and drive head-on into one of the trees. Your car won't stand it, and you probably won't live to tell the tale. Nevertheless, the shock is somewhat comparable to what happens when a light tank hits a solid obstacle. Of course, the tree gives and the weight of the tank carries through, so it is not quite so bad. After your collision with the tree, if you still desire further tank experience, find a cut bank somewhere, 10ft high with an angle of perhaps 100 percent drop. Now drive right over it at high speed and let your car jump down. Your sensations will be many and very comparable to the feelings of the man in a tank. But the great steadiness of weight possessed by the tank comes to his aid. In some manner, his steel monster is made to stand the punishment and your car isn't.

"Furthermore, on the inside of his tank are nice, thick rubber pads, placed everywhere that his head may come in contact with the steel interior. The tank man wears a shock helmet which is guaranteed to withstand concussion—that is, if anything on earth will. It is more protective than the football player's headgear and as effective as the helmet worn by air crews. In spite of all this, a man in a tank is occasionally knocked unconscious or breaks an arm.

"If you desire further proof as to the joys of a tank ride, drive what's left of your car back to the smooth lawn. Get one of your neigh-

Every tank has limits to the amount of armor protection it can carry. When it meets a weapon that overmatches its level of protection, the result can be catastrophic for both the vehicle and crew. This

German WWII-era Mk. IV medium tank has been completely blown apart by internal explosions of its onboard ammunition and fuel. *National Archives*

bors out in his car and arrange a jousting match, such as was indulged in by the armored knights of old. Each of you back off to opposite ends of the lawn. Charge each other as fast as your cars will go and meet head-on. Of course, unfortunately, when you have done this, all sense of similarity to a tank ride will be gone because you will be unconscious. Nevertheless, tanks do meet head-on in battle. When they do, I don't know what happens.

"There is one comparison you cannot get from your car, and that is getting into and out of a tank. This requires long practice, athletic agility, and mountain-climbing experience. But all in all, a tank trip over moderately rough ground is amazingly smooth riding. Even in bad going, you are surprised that you are not thrown about more. Of course, when your monster climbs up a 10ft obstacle and jumps off into space on the other side, you are sure you have come to the end of your rope.

"The accelerator and gearshift of a tank are much the same as those in your car. However, the steering is different. Instead of a wheel, most tanks contain an individual stick or lever on the caterpillar tread on either side, one controlling the left and the other the right caterpillar track. You work both of these, one with each hand, to navigate the monster. Seasoned men of the tank service say it becomes easy. The noise is so great that the tank commander, standing in the turret, directs the driver by touching him with his feet; word-of-mouth commands are impossible. Again, experienced tank men tell me that, if you learn to relax as you do in riding a horse, you become accustomed to the tank's movement, whether it is a long swing or a sharp bronco-like buck. If you are standing in the turret, all the swings are much wider and more difficult at first. I understand that expert tank drivers can handle their machines, the small and

Typical examples of the type of AFVs built in large numbers by the Soviets in the postwar-era are these two T54 main battle tanks. Armed with a 100mm gun and having a four-man crew, the vehicle has not done well in combat. *Michael Green*

medium types, almost as if they were polo ponies, boasting that they can stop and turn on a dime.

"The narrow slit openings in the sides and front of the tank, though they may exclude bullets, do nothing toward keeping out dust. Thus, when you are in the midst of the charge of the tank brigade, hurtling across the terrain, you may find that you can neither see nor breathe because of the dust—but this won't stop the armored division, for the tank men have goggles especially made for such occasions, and if necessary they don their dust masks.

"Merely to look at a tank brigade tempts you to try to visualize it in battle. Perhaps you can imagine several hundred of these modern steel battleships of the land, charging at top speed, all throttles and all guns wide open.

Their own noise is deadening and deafening enough, but it is merged with and magnified beyond description by the roar of continuous explosions. I cannot describe such a battle with justice. I doubt if Dante could. From in the rear of the tanks comes the thunder of their own artillery; from in front, their enemy's. There is a shrieking, whining flat canopy of shells overhead, their own and their enemy's. The drone and scream of many airplanes is also continuous, punctuated by the soul-racking crash and explosion of great bombs. In the midst of all this, you must imagine the constant impact and crashing explosion as burning planes collide with the earth. The morally wounded tank is thrown on its side by shell or bomb. Then immediately follows the explosion of gas tanks and unused ammunition. The steel monster is tossed

The British-built Centurion tank developed right at the end of WWII was one of the most successful postwar tanks for many decades. Heavily modified and upgraded over its operational life, the Centuri-on best embodied the three main characteristics of tank design: firepower, armor protection, and mobility. The vehicle pictured is from the Israeli Army. *Israeli Army*

29

This WWII-era picture clearly illustrates the differences in size among a light, medium, and heavy tank. While both the M5 American light tank and the M4 Sherman medium tank saw use during the war years, the M6 heavy tank never went into series production. No M6 tanks are known to have survived. *US Army*

high in the air to its destruction by an exploding huge land mine. The moans of the dying and shrieks of the wounded are drowned out in this unearthly din. When Sherman said, 'War is hell,' he knew nothing about 'hell on wheels'."

Tank Components

Most tanks since WWII can be divided into three major components: the hull, the turret, and the tracked suspension system. A tank hull is typically divided into two compartments: the driver's compartment and the engine compartment. The engine is normally compartmentalized to reduce the chance of a fuel fire spreading into the crew area. Tank engines are normally located in the rear of the vehicle, along with the transmission. Exceptions to this rule can be found in the Swedish S-tank and the Israeli Merkava tank. While many WWII tanks had gas engines, most modern tanks have high-performance diesel engines or, in the case of the American Abrams tank, a gas-turbine engine.

The turret of a tank tends to be fitted in the middle of the vehicle's hull. It's in the turret that the main striking power is mounted. The cannon or primary armament is typically a high-velocity gun that can fire both armor-defeating high-explosive and smoke projectiles. It is operated by a gunner and a loader (some newer tanks have automatic loaders), and either the gunner or tank commander controls the firing. In addition to the cannon and the men, the turret will contain all the fire-control equipment, vision devices, and ammunition for both the cannon and machine guns. Most tanks have a machine gun fitted alongside the main gun. This gun may be fired either simultaneously with, or independently of, the tank gun. This weapon is most effective against personnel and unarmored vehicles at ranges up to 1000yd.

For close-in defense against aircraft and attack helicopters, tanks normally are armed with a second, larger-caliber machine gun. Most American tanks from WWII on have been fitted on the top of their turrets with at least one .50cal machine gun. It was normally controlled by the tank commander. Because of its high muzzle velocity (speed to the target), this machine gun is also very effective against lightly armored enemy vehicles.

Tank turrets are usually traversed by electric or hydraulic devices. Some older tanks, especially from WWII, had their turrets turned by hand cranks, a very slow and tiring process for any tank crewman.

For better visibility, tank drivers are always located in the front hulls . In older-generation tanks from WWII and before, there were sometimes two drivers because of the tiring nature of controlling such a heavy vehicle. An assistant driver would also be equipped with a hull-mounted machine gun

firing forward. In postwar tank designs, this position was eliminated because of the space it took up. Most tanks now have only a single driver, giving them a crew of four: driver, gunner, loader, and vehicle commander. In contrast, some World War I tanks had a crew of from eight to twenty-four.

Most AFVs must depend on a fully tracked suspension system to distribute their weight evenly over a large area of soft ground. Without tracks, a tank mounted on wheels would quickly sink into the ground because its weight would not be supported by a sufficiently large enough area of contact. Tracks are like snowshoes for people. Without the snowshoes, a person would be unable to cross certain types of soft snow. With them, that person can cross over soft snow because his or her weight is more evenly distributed.

Originally only hinged metal plates on the first agricultural tractors, tracks evolved into combined steel and rubber blocks or just steel

The Panther medium tank was considered one of the best German tanks of WWII. Like all other tanks, its mobility was limited. The Panther tank pictured and a second vehicle located behind it have both become mired in soft ground and were easy targets for Allied gunners. *National Archives*

blocks connected together in a long belt that would run around a series of rubber-tipped steel road wheels located on either side of a tank's hull. These two long belts of blocks linked together to form a track area aligned parallel with the ground. The bottom portion of the tracks ride on the ground and provide an area large enough to support the weight of the tank. Tanks with rubber-blocked steel tracks are the most popular among collectors since they may be operated on city streets. All steel tracks on tanks tend to tear up pavement and are very unpopular with local city gov-ernments, counties, and neighbors—so permits are necessary.

The power to move the tank and its tracks is transmitted from the engine and by large sprockets, normally located at the rear. These sprockets engage the tracks with steel toes that make them move in a continuous loop around the numerous supporting wheels found on either side of the tank hull. The tracks themselves are nothing more than a portable roadway for the tank's wheels to run over. As the rear wheels of the tank cross over the tracks, the rear sprockets pick them up and carry them forward along the top side of the hull and re-lays them in front of the vehicle to be driven over again.

Armored Cars

Besides tanks, there are a number of other AFVs that are collected. The most well-known of these are armored cars. Often confused with tanks because many of them have turrets with direct-fire weapons, armored cars actually saw combat before the first tank was ever built. In the early days, armored cars were designed primarily as high-speed road vehicles. More modern armored cars on the other hand can almost match the off-road mobility of fully tracked vehicles. Newer cannon technol-

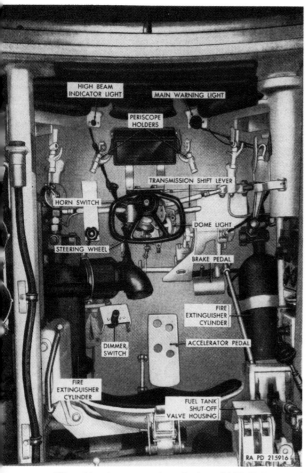

The driver's compartment of an M48 Patton tank, with all its various components listed. *US Army*

An overhead shot of the engine compartment of an early-model M48 Patton medium tank. Early Patton tanks all had gasoline engines, which meant they had a short range. When the M48A3 Patton was built, it was updated with a diesel engine that doubled its range. *US Army*

This side view of a British-built Centurion tank in Israeli military service shows the arrangement of a typical Western tank's suspension system. The power to move the vehicle is provided by the large sprockets at the rear of the hull. Located above the paired rubber-tipped steel road wheels are the smaller support wheels that carry the vehicle's track forward along the top side of the hull and relay it in front of the vehicle to be driven over. *Israeli Army*

ogy has also given some armored cars the firepower of WWII-era tanks.

While their mobility and firepower have improved over the years, wheeled vehicles are still unable to carry the same amount of armor protection as found on fully tracked AFVs. As a result, armored cars have generally been restricted to reconnaissance and security missions, where their thinner armor is less of a problem. Because they weigh less than tanks, they can cross bridges that would collapse under the weight of fully tracked vehicles. Wheeled AFVs are also cheaper to build and maintain than their fully tracked counterparts.

To achieve off-road mobility, armored cars tend to have multi-wheel drive and independent suspension systems. The simplest and cheapest armored cars are four-wheel-drive vehicles. However, they have very little ground contact area on which to distribute their weight and they tend to get stuck in soft soil. To overcome this problem, designers have built vehicles with as many as eight wheels. Unfortunately, this boosts the vehicles' size, and on the battlefield, smaller is normally better. The harder you are to see, the less likely you are going to be shot at, an important feature for a reconnaissance (scouting) vehicle.

Armored reconnaissance vehicles (ARVs) can also be fully tracked. The difficult question then becomes: What is the difference between a light tank used as a reconnaissance vehicle and a full-fledged main battle tank? To compound the confusion, many modern fully tracked infantry fighting vehicles can be configured as reconnaissance vehicles yet are outwardly similar to the standard vehicle.

The distinction between different types of AFVs is sometimes very difficult to make, even among the armies that use them. In war, the soldiers who operate the vehicles don't always make these fine distinctions and use whatever they have at the moment, regardless of what the original designers may have intended.

Armored Personnel Carriers

As early as World War I, the British Army had experimented with modifying tanks to carry infantry. However, it was left to the German Army of WWII to pioneer the use of mechanized armored transport vehicles. While many other armies before the outbreak of WWII had provided their infantry with unarmored trucks, their very poor cross-country mobility made them unable to follow fully tracked AFVs. The German and American armies' answer to this problem was to build large numbers of armored half-tracks. They were relatively inexpensive to build in large numbers, but both the American and German soldiers quickly found out that their armored half-tracks still could not keep pace with their tanks. Being thinly armored and open-topped, the half-tracks also proved to be very vulnerable to small arms and artillery fire. In late 1944, British and Canadian Army units in Western Europe decided their infantry units needed full-tracked mobility. Their answer was to convert a number of tanks and self-propelled artillery guns into infantry personnel carriers. Tank turrets were removed, producing a large opening in the tank's hull in which the soldiers could ride. The main armament was removed on fully tracked, self-propelled artillery guns, and the resulting space could carry up to a squad of ten infantrymen. While these fully tracked vehicles offered su-

To match the off-road mobility of fully tracked vehicles such as tanks, armored car designers have been forced to use as many as eight multidriven wheels. During WWII, the German Army deployed a large number of multiwheeled armored cars. Pictured is a captured German eight-wheeled armored car mounting a short-barreled 75mm gun in its open-topped superstructure. *US Army*

perior cross-country mobility to the half-tracks then in use, they were still open-topped. It wasn't until after WWII that the major armies of the world started to build large numbers of fully armored, fully tracked, and wheeled APCs.

Most APCs built since the end of WWII through the 1960s were basically very simple, thinly armored boxes used as battlefield taxis. Armed only with machine guns for self-protection, they were designed only to deliver their troops to the battlefield, where they would dismount and then march into combat. Many of these early postwar generation of APCs can be found on the collectors' market.

Beginning in the 1970s, the Soviet and West German armies began to deploy fully tracked heavily armed infantry fighting vehicles. While their main purpose was still to carry infantry into battle, they were now given the job of following the tanks right onto the enemy objective and to then fight along-side the tanks. To do this, these infantry fight-ing vehicles were fitted with both small-cal-iber cannons and antitank missiles. Compared to the earlier generation APCs, these new infantry fighting vehicles had much thicker armor protection.

The US Army didn't deploy a comparable infantry fighting vehicle until the early 1980s, when the M2 Bradley entered its inventory. Armed with a 25mm cannon in a two-man turret, the M2 Bradley was also fitted with an antitank missile launcher. The crew could fire personal weapons through ports in the vehicle's hull.

Because infantry fighting vehicles and most modern tanks are so costly, they will re-main in military use for a long time to come. And when they are released, their associated maintenance needs may make it very hard for a private collector to keep such a vehicle.

Miscellaneous Armored Vehicles

As soon as the tank was developed, de-signers sought to produce support vehicles

The best-known APC built since WWII is the fully tracked M113. With almost 90,000 various versions built since 1960, the M113 is in service in more than twenty-five different countries' armies. *FMC Corporation*

The Army's most modern self-propelled gun mounted on an armored, fully tracked chassis is the M109A3 pictured in Saudi Arabia prior to Operation Desert Storm. The M109 series is very typical in overall design to other countries' self-propelled guns. *US Army*

with the same mobility. One of the earliest vehicles developed to support the tank with indirect fire was the self-propelled gun mounted on an armored, fully tracked chassis. Unlike a tank which mounts a direct-fire weapon, a self-propelled gun is an artillery weapon that normally fires at targets outside its line-of-sight. While tanks and self-propelled guns look very similar externally, self-propelled guns do not have the same amount of armor protection as tanks do, since they are not supposed to operate on the front lines. Artillery weapons mounted in self-propelled guns are typically much larger than those found in tanks and usually require a much larger crew.

Self-propelled guns were not used on a full-scale basis until WWII. The Germans were the first to use them in combat and were soon copied by other armies. Most self-propelled guns used during WWII were based on converted tank chassis. As a result, they normally did not feature any overhead protection

for their crews. As technology improved after WWII, designers gave them both overhead protection and during the 1960s, full 360deg traversable turrets.

As ground-attack aircraft became more of a threat to tanks and other AFVs during WWII, numerous armies began to mount antiaircraft guns on converted tanks, half-tracks, and armored cars. After WWII, as jet fighters took to the skies in large numbers, these antiaircraft guns were replaced by antiaircraft missiles in most modern armies.

When tanks or any other AFVs break down or are put out of commission due to battle damage, armies needed some way to recover them. Normal practice in the past and even today is to convert tanks into tank-recovery vehicles. Equipped with cranes, winches, and bulldozer blades, these vehicles can travel anywhere a tank can. Some private collectors have also bought tank-recovery vehicles to recover any of their own vehicles when necessary.

A very modern form of antiaircraft vehicle is this West German Army Gepard. Based on the armored chassis of the Leopard 1 tank, the Gepard is armed with two 35mm guns attached to a surveillance radar. *Michael Green*

Chapter 3

Tanks

Six-Ton M1917

The oldest AFV in collectors' hands today is the American-built Six-Ton M1917 light tank. Copied from a French design, about 1,000 of these vehicles were built by various contractors between 1918 and 1919. Because World War I ended in 1918, none of these American-built light tanks saw combat. American troops had to depend on French- and British-supplied tanks.

The Six-Ton had a two-man crew, a driver in the front hull and a vehicle comman-

der/gunner in the turret. There were no tank intercom systems; instead, the vehicle commander, who sat directly behind and above the driver, would use his feet to direct the driver in the direction he wanted the vehicle to go. A tap on the left shoulder meant a left turn, a tap on the right shoulder meant a right turn, and a tap on the driver's back meant go forward or stop. In combat, going across rough terrain, this system of communication must have been very painful for the driver if the tank commander got too excited. Since ra-

The American-built Six Ton M1917 light tank was a copy of the World War I-era French-built Renault light tank. Pictured are a formation of French-built Renault light tanks during a training exercise. *Patton Museum*

Displayed at the Patton Museum of Armor and Cavalry in Fort Knox, Kentucky, is this preserved example of the Army Six Ton M1917 light tank. *Michael Green*

dios had not yet been installed in most tanks of the period, tank crews usually depended on signal flags to pass on orders from one tank to another.

The Six-Ton M1917 was armed with either a very short-barrel 37mm cannon or a single .30cal machine gun in a fully 360deg one-man traversable turret. This was the first tank in military service to feature such a turret. Most other tanks of the World War I-era had hull-mounted cannons and machine guns. Armor on the vehicle was no thicker than 1/4in at its thickest.

The Six-Ton M1917 weighed 7.25 tons fully loaded, and was powered by a Buda four-cylinder, 42hp, water-cooled gas engine. Top speed was 5.5mph, and the maximum operational range was 30 miles. The transmission was the sliding gear type with four speeds forward and one reverse. The tank could cross a 7ft trench, a 2ft stream, or a 35deg slope. It could knock down a 3ft vertical wall or trees up to 8in thick.

Because of a lack of funding for tank development after World War I, the obsolete Six-Ton M1917 soldiered on into the 1930s. A large number of Six-Ton tanks were later taken out of mothball and supplied to the Canadian Army as training tanks in1940. Once the Canadians got newer tanks, the Six-Ton M1917 light tanks were retired and later scrapped. Some vehicles were preserved as monuments or in museum collections. Hollywood also acquired at least one Six-Ton tank, which appeared in a number of films made during the thirties. Six of these tanks are now in collectors' hands. At least two of them have been restored to running condition. Prices for a Six-Ton tank (when available) can range from $25,000 for a hulk to $45,000 for an operational vehicle. Since many parts and important components are impossible to find today, a fully restored vehicle could cost as much as $75,000.

M3 Lee and Grant Medium Tanks

When Germany invaded and overran both Poland (1939) and France (1940), one of its medium tanks mounted a short-barrel, low-velocity, 75mm cannon in a large three-man turret, with 360deg transverse. Known as the Mk. IV, this German medium tank had a dramatic effect on future American tank design. Prior to the German attacks on Poland and France, the Army had spent most of its time and limited funds on developing a number of light tanks armed mainly with machine guns.

This is not to say that the US Army completely ignored the medium tank. In late 1936, the Army recommended the development of the T5 medium tank. The T5 was essentially an enlarged version of the Army's M3 light tank. Using many of the same components found on the M3 light tank, the T5 was supposed to have more firepower and armor protection than other American tanks then in service. Starting in early 1939, a number of T5 prototype tanks were tested with a combination of different cannons and machine guns. Standardized in late 1939 as the M2 and

Pictured during a training exercise in the United States during WWII is this late-model cast-hull M3 Lee medium tank. It was armed with both a 37mm cannon mounted in a 360deg traversable turret and a hull-mounted 75mm cannon. *US Army*

M2A1 medium tank and armed with a 37mm cannon and six machine guns, this vehicle proved to be the beginnings of the M4 Sherman tank, which would reach production five years later.

On August 15, 1940, the Army entered into a contract with Chrysler Corporation for the production of 1,000 M2A1 23-ton medium tanks at the rate of 100 a month.

Reports from Europe indicated that the M2A1 would be obsolete before it was built. On August 28, 1940, the Army abruptly canceled the contract for the M2A1 and asked Chrysler to build 1,000 new, as-yet-undesigned M3 medium tanks with thicker armor than the M2A1 and armed with a 75mm gun, like the German Army Mk. IV medium tank.

Because the machines and skills needed to build a large turret mounting a 75mm gun did not exist in the United States and would take time to develop, the Army decided to adopt a tank design with a hull-mounted 75mm gun. The Army had already developed an experimental design based on the T5 medium tank but mounting a 75mm howitzer. Known as the T5E2, this vehicle featured the 75mm howitzer in the right front of the vehicle's hull, a setup tested to be practical for tank installation.

When built, the M3 was fitted with a 75mm cannon in a limited traverse mounting on the right side of the front hull sponson. A 37mm cannon was carried in a fully traversing turret on top of the vehicle's box-like superstructure, which itself was built out of a combination of cast- and welded-steel armored plates riveted together. Later variants of the M3 featured numerous production differences, including a cast-steel hull.

The M3 weighed nearly 30 tons, and was originally designed to carry a crew of seven: the vehicle commander, a driver, two loaders, two gunners, and a radioman. For secondary armament, it was fitted with four machine guns, two in the hull firing forward and two in the 37mm cannon-armed turret. One was mounted alongside the 37mm cannon, the other on a large cupola on top of the vehicle. Overall height of the M3 was 10ft 3in.

The first-production model M3 tanks were powered by the nine-cylinder Curtiss-Wright radial air-cooled gas aircraft engine. Later models of the M3 were fitted with either General Motors (GM) diesel water-cooled engines or a thirty-cylinder Chrysler multibank gas engine.

The final design work on the M3 was finished in February 1941, and by August of that same year, full-scale production had begun. A total of 4,924 M3s were built until August 1942.

The British Army, which lost the bulk of its tanks during the evacuation at Dunkirk, France, was a big user of the M3. Since British industry did not have the ability to mass-produce new tanks to replace its losses, the British Army bought more than 660 modified M3 tanks with a different 37mm gun turret. The British designation for its version of the American M3 was the General Grant. The Americans referred to their M3s as the General Lee. The British-modified M3 tanks first saw action in North Africa on May 27, 1942, when the famous Gen. Erwin Rommel (the "Desert Fox") launched an attack on British forces stationed near the small desert town of Bir Hacheim. The 75mm cannon on the British Grant tanks could out-range the German Mk. III medium tank fitted with a 50mm cannon or the larger Mk. IV tank fitted with a short-barreled 75mm cannon.

Army units first saw action with their M3s on November 28, 1942, when, in conjunction with a British Army unit, they were given the job of taking control of a small town in Tunisia, North Africa, and a nearby airfield held by German forces. During the attack, American M3s suffered serious losses from hidden German antitank guns. Over the next few days, the green American tankers suf-

Pictured is the American-built M3 medium tank supplied to the British Army during WWII under contract. The British M3 medium tank was named the Grant and featured a larger turret on top of the hull. *British Army photo*

fered additional heavy losses at the hands of the more-experienced German troops.

Shortly after this series of battles and subsequent actions during the fighting at Kasserine Pass, the M3 Lee tanks were quickly replaced by newly arrived M4 Sherman tanks. Some M3 Lee tanks served the remainder of the war fighting the Japanese in the Pacific and Far East. With little to fear from obsolete Japanese tanks, the M3 served with British, American, and Australian units. About 1,300 M3 medium tanks were shipped to the USSR under the Lend-Lease program.

The M3 tank had a number of serious shortcomings. With the traverse of its hull-mounted 75mm gun limited, the entire tank had to be turned if an enemy vehicle appeared almost anywhere but right in front of the main gun. The 75mm main gun also had a very low muzzle velocity, which meant that its shells couldn't always penetrate the armor of enemy tanks. Combined with inadequate armor protection due to the poor arrangement and riveted construction of the vehicle armor plates, the Army was very anxious to field the Sherman tank, which was designed to correct these deficiencies.

There are two restored examples of the M3 medium tank now in private hands. These vehicles were brought from Australia, where many rare old WWII AFVs have been found recently. It is reported that Brazil also has a small number of surplus M3 Lees, which both military museums and collectors have tried to acquire. Prices for a hulk could start at around $30,000.00, with an operational vehicle going

The best-known American tank of WWII was the M4 Sherman. Almost 50,000 were built between 1942 and 1945. It also saw service with a number of wartime Allied armies. Pictured are a couple of very early M4A1 Shermans on parade in an American city. It is estimated that over 800 Shermans of various models have survived to the present day. *US Army*

for $45,000.00 to $50,000.00 A fully restored vehicle could bring up to $75,000.00. According to most American and British tankers who served in either the Lee and the Grant during WWII, they were difficult vehicles to drive and maintain.

M4 Sherman Medium Tank

The best known American tank ever built is probably the M4 Sherman series, of which almost 50,000 were produced between 1942 and 1945. It was the mainstay of not only the American forces during WWII but also of many different Allied armies.

The M4 was considered to be a very durable, reliable vehicle, and easy to build in large numbers; the biggest production problem was the lack of enough engines to power all the Shermans being built. Because of the different engines and other details, there were a number of variants fielded, including the M4, M4A1, M4A2, M4A3, M4A4, and M4A6. Originally, it was intended that all Sherman tanks have a cast-steel hull and turret, but the lack of casting facilities caused many to be built with a box-like welded-steel armored hull. It was this welded hull version of the Sherman powered by a Ford gas engine (GAA) known as the M4A3 Sherman that proved to be the most popular version with the Army. Unfortunately, there were not enough of these engines. Many Army Shermans, including the M4 and M4A1, were fitted with modified radial gas aircraft-type engines. The M4A2 and M4A6 variants had diesel engines. Since the American military wanted only gas-powered tanks during WWII, most of the diesel-powered Sherman tanks were supplied to other Allied armies, especially the British and Soviet armies.

The first-generation Shermans were all armed with a 75mm gun. Later versions were armed with a 76mm gun. Neither weapon proved capable of dealing with later-war German tanks such as the Panther or Tiger. It was the British Army that mounted a very long 17-pounder antitank gun in a Sherman turret, greatly improving the Allied armies' ability to destroy German tanks.

Another serious shortcoming in the design of the Sherman tank was its very thin armor. Combined with its relatively tall and somewhat box-like shape, the Sherman proved to be very vulnerable to a wide range of enemy antitank weapons. In response, Sherman tankers tended to cover their vehicles with anything that could offer a little extra ballistic

The M4 Sherman series of medium tanks weighed about 34 tons. Most early Shermans built were armed with a 75mm cannon and at least three machine guns. They had five-men crews: The driver and assistant driver rode in the front hull and the commander, gunner, and loader rode in the turret. *US Army*

To increase the firepower of the M4 Sherman tank series, the Army began mounting a 76mm cannon. Pictured side-by-side are two Sherman tanks. The one on the left is armed with a 76mm cannon, and the one on the right is fitted with the earlier 75mm cannon. Both these vehicles belong to a private collector. *Michael Green*

The best-known postwar user of American-built Sherman tanks in combat was the Israeli Army. In an attempt to upgrade its combat effectiveness, the Israeli Army fitted a French 75mm high-velocity cannon in the turret and replaced the original gas engine with a modern diesel one. Eventually, the Israeli Army replaced their Shermans with more modern tanks. Several of these Israeli-modified Shermans have passed into collectors' hands. Pictured is an Israeli Super Sherman with a 75mm cannon, belonging to a private collector. *Michael Green*

protection from enemy weapons. The Army also added a number of extra welded armor plates to production-line Shermans.

WWII-era Sherman tanks weighed in at about 34 tons fully loaded. They were 9ft 7in tall, 8ft 9in wide, and about 21ft long. In comparison, the Army's current main battle tank, the M1A1 Abrams, weighs in approximately 70 tons fully loaded, is 7ft 7in tall and 11ft 8in wide.

The basis for the Sherman tank was the earlier M3 medium tank, equipped with a 75mm main gun mounted in its hull, which produced very limited traverse ability. The entire tank had to be turned for the main gun to be fired. In tank battles, the vehicle getting off the first shot is usually the winner. The M3 also had a very high silhouette and poor armor protection, a deadly combination in combat.

The M4 Sherman was designed to correct M3 deficiencies. The 75mm main gun was now mounted in a 360deg traversable turret. The early vehicles rode on a volute-spring suspension system, combined with steel and rubber tracks. A life of 3,000 miles was not unusual for these Sherman tank tracks. German steel tracks of WWII could last 600 miles at the most.

During the course of WWII, the M4 Sherman tank series underwent continual development until it emerged in 1945 as the M4A3E8 (Easy Eight) Sherman in American military service. This final version had a 76mm high-velocity gun, improved suspension with wider tracks, and a Ford GAA gas engine. The last Sherman was phased out of American military service in 1956.

After WWII, the Sherman saw combat against Soviet-built tanks in the Korean War. The Sherman's most successful combat action was in the service of the Israeli Army from the 1956 War through the 1973 Yom Kippur War. The Israeli Army wasted no time in putting the most powerful engine it could fit in the Sherman hull, as well as arming it with the most powerful gun it could find. The first was a French copy of the 75mm gun from the WWII Panther tank. Later versions featured a French-designed 105mm gun. With these upgraded Shermans, Israel's Army normally bested the large fleets of more modern Soviet-built tanks supplied to Israel's Arab neighbors.

While replaced in American military service by newer generations of vehicles, the M4 Sherman series has continued to serve in countless numbers of armies around the world. From Africa to South America, from Japan to the Middle East, the Sherman tank has only during the last decade begun to slowly fade from army inventories. Israel, the biggest postwar user of Sherman tanks, retired its last vehicle in the late 1970s. Many of the surplus Israeli Sherman tanks are now appearing on the collectors' market.

The biggest advantage to owning a Sherman is the wide availability of many parts and the existence of dealers to supply them. Having access to these parts allows a collector to have a vehicle that he can operate to his heart's content. This is in sharp contrast to many other rarer AFVs, for which parts are no longer available.

Though parts are available to keep them running, Shermans are not pleasant vehicles to drive. They have unboosted steering controls and the transmissions and clutches are hard to push. According to AFV collector Jacques M. Littlefield, "The Sherman tank is the worse vehicle to drive for any length of time, even trying to park one will leave you in a sweat."

Because of the Sherman's weight and size, the owner needs a special permit to trailer it anywhere.

The most desired engine for the Sherman collector, is the Ford GAA engine because the engine runs so well. However, the Ford GAA engine is not as easy to work on or to find as the twin GM diesels fitted into the M4A2 Shermans. The only problem with any twin-engine vehicle, is you can count on twice the number of automotive headaches when things go wrong.

Also fairly easy to find are the modified radial gas engines found in the M4 and M4A1 Shermans. The disadvantages of this type of engine are many. The radial has very poor torque characteristics, making it somewhat underpowered in rough going and very easy to stall. To start the radial engine powered vehicle you have to turn a large hand crank located in the rear of the tank at least sixty times to make sure that you get the oil out of the bottom cyclinders.

The most difficult to find Sherman engine is the Chrysler A57 Multibank. Made of six now-discontinued car engines, the Chrysler A57 was considered such a maintenance headache by the US Army during WWII, that they gave almost all of them away to the British. The British Army found that a well-trained crew could keep the vehicle running fairly well. An individual collector, on the

After WWII, the Soviets widely exported the T34 to several countries, including the various Arab countries arrayed against Israel. Unfortunately, the T34 in Arab hands didn't perform well in combat. The vehicle pictured in a 1957 parade in Israel is a captured T34. *Israeli Army*

The most important Soviet tank built during WWII was the T34 medium tank. Originally armed with a 76.2mm cannon, most models produced from 1944 throughout the postwar years mounted an 85mm cannon. The T34 pictured is armed with an 85mm cannon and was used as a training aid at Fort Ord, California, for many years. *Michael Green*

other hand, may not have the time and parts to keep a six-engine powered vehicle in top operating condition.

There are at least 50 or more WWII-era Sherman tanks now in collectors' hands. They consist of a variety of different types. The greatest number seem to be the M4A1 cast-hull Sherman equipped with the radial engine. There are also a growing number of Israeli-modified Shermans, powered by American 460hp. Cummins diesel engines, which have entered the collector's marketplace in recent years.

Prices on Shermans tend to be fairly stable. Hulks start at $20,000, with operational vehicles going for $50,000. In prime restored condition a Sherman could go for as much as $75,000.

Soviet T34 Medium Tank

The best known Soviet tank ever built has to be the T34 medium tank series. First rolling off the factory floor in September 1940, improved models of this vehicle can still be found in the inventory of some Third World armies. With almost 50,000 T34 series tanks built during and after WWII by Soviet, Polish, and Czech factories, the vehicle was widely exported to countries with governments friendly to the Communist cause. As a result, the T34 saw combat with a wide variety of different armies from the Far East to the Middle East. It's only been during the last decade that the T34 series has finally been replaced by newer generations of tanks. In Soviet service, the T34 series was only used in training units after the 1960s.

When first built in 1940, the T34 had the most innovative tank design of its day. In most respects, the vehicle was far superior to anything the Germans had built before then. While most other countries' tanks were still built in square box-like shapes, the T34 designers were the first to make full use of the principle that well-sloped armor adds greatly to its effectiveness. The T34's front plate sloped at 60deg up over the driver's position, but was pierced on the left with the driver's hatch (fitted with a periscope) and on the right for a ball-mounted machine gun. The sides of the T34 hull were sloped at 41deg, the rear at 49deg. Armor thickness on the T34 hulls and turrets averaged 2in. When first built, the T34 was armed with a 76.2mm gun in a welded-steel armor turret with sloping sides. Later versions of the T34 series were armed with an 85mm gun in a cast-steel armor turret. The performance of this 85mm gun was approximately similar to that of the German 88mm used in the Tiger I tank.

The typical T34 series tank was 20ft 4in long, 9ft 7in wide, and about 7ft 10in tall. Powered by a twelve-cylinder, water-cooled diesel engine, the T34 had a top speed of about 31mph and an operational range of 186 miles. With a very high power-to-weight ratio and very wide tracks, the T34 tank had outstanding cross-country mobility. Weighing in at the 35-ton range, the T34 was called the "Snow King" by German soldiers because of its ability at high speeds to cross thick snow that would bog down German tanks.

When the T34 first saw combat against the German Army in the summer of 1941, it was a complete surprise. The Germans had nothing in their weapons inventory that could stop the T34 except the 88mm antiaircraft gun. So impressed with the T34 tank were the German soldiers that many asked that German factories copy it. This wasn't technically possible, but it did result in the Germans building both the Tiger and Panther tanks. These German tanks were individually superior to the T34, but German industry could never build enough of them to stop the large numbers of T34s built.

The T34 was not a perfect tank. Transmission problems plagued early models. They were very uncomfortable to drive and to op-

erate for long periods of time. Poor tactical use by Soviet tankers and their commanders also contributed to very high losses of T34 tanks throughout WWII. Early T34s also had a two-man turret crew, compared to the three-man crew of German and American medium tanks. This meant that the early T34 had only a vehicle commander and gunner. The Soviet tank commander not only had to direct his tank and its movements with other tanks, but also had to load the main gun and the coaxial machine gun mounted along side of it. German and American tanks had a full-time loader, freeing the vehicle commander to concentrate on more important things. To make matters worse, the early T34s did not have a turret basket. The turret crew sat on small stools suspended from the turret ring. In combat, with the tank's floor covered with hot empty shell cases and open bins, it was very hard for the crew to function without injury. Even later when the Soviets developed an improved three-man turret, the T34 crew was handicapped by very crude fire-control devices. With their superior fire-control systems, German tanks could normally fire effectively at T34 tanks long before they could return accurate fire themselves. These shortcomings also placed the T34 tank at a disadvantage in postwar conflicts, where superior

Most German Tiger tanks saw action on the Russian front. Faced with larger numbers of Soviet tanks, the long-range 88mm cannon, combined with a superior fire-control system, allowed the Tiger crews to destroy large numbers of Soviet tanks in combat. *German Army*

Western-built tanks normally would get the first shot in before the T34 could engage in firing.

During the 1960s, many old T34 tanks that had been placed into storage were rebuilt using the engine and wheel components from the T54 series of Soviet tanks. These vehicles and upgraded Polish, Czech, and even Chinese T34 tanks have recently begun to appear in private hands. There are no early T34s with the 76.2mm gun except in museums. All models of the T34 in private hands have the 85mm gun mounted in a three-man turret.

For the collector, the T34 tank has a lot of positive features. It's a fairly simple and straightforward design with a rugged engine and transmission. Most of the vehicle's automotive components are easy to work on, with the exception of the air cleaners. On the nega-

tive side, the T34 is very tiring to drive. At low speeds it can be moved around fairly easily. At speeds over 10mph the vehicle becomes harder to steer and turn. Trying to shift takes a lot of strength and energy. During WWII, it was reported that Russian tankers used small hammers to help them get the shift lever into gear. Being an older generation vehicle, parts availability could be a problem in the future as most vehicles are junked.

With the end of the Cold War, thousands of T34s have become surplus to the armies of the former Warsaw Pact. Most are being cut up for scrap as required by treaty. At least fifty T34s have been bought by dealers for sale to collectors. The base price for a hulk runs about $15,000. An operational vehicle should range around $25,000. Top price for a fully restored vehicle could reach $35,000.

The best German heavy tank of WWII was the Tiger. Protected by thick steel armor and armed with a very powerful 88mm cannon, the Tiger took a heavy toll of American and Allied tanks through-out the war years. This vehicle pictured at Aberdeen Proving Ground, Maryland, is currently on loan to a German museum. *Richard Cox*

German Tiger Heavy Tank

The best known and most feared German tank of WWII was the Tiger I. Protected by very thick armor and fitted with a powerful 88mm main gun, the Tiger I could punch holes through any Allied tank. The Tiger I fought with distinction in North Africa, the USSR, and throughout Western and Eastern Europe until Nazi Germany finally surrendered in 1945.

The battle-ready Tiger I weighed 56 tons. By comparison, the US M4 Sherman weighed about 34 tons, and the British Cromwell weighed 28 tons. (The Tiger's battle companion, the Panther, weighed 45 tons.) Most of the Tiger's weight was in its immensely thick armor plating.

Power to move this 56-ton behemoth and to operate its systems came from a Maybach water-cooled V-12 gas engine rated at 642hp at 3,000rpm. The 20-ton turret drive was hydraulic, but could be operated by hand, although hand operation required 720 turns of the gunner's traverse wheel and 595 turns of the commander's wheel to make a complete traverse.

The Tiger's suspension was unique in that it used torsion bars and interleaved road wheels, twenty-four on each side. This wheel arrangement was the Tiger's visually distinguishing feature. To meet European standards for rail transport, the outer four wheels on each side had to be removed and narrow, 20in-wide tracks were fitted. The battle tracks were 28in wide, giving a ground pressure on the order of 14.7lb per square inch.

The first 495 Tigers were fitted for total submersion to a depth of 15ft. Inflatable rubber rings and fittings sealed the hull openings, and a 13ft snorkel air intake was added. Succeeding Tigers were not equipped for total submersion but could ford 4ft-deep streams.

The Tiger had a five-man crew: commander, gunner, loader, driver, and hull machine-gunner/radio man.

This superb tank was both time-consuming and expensive to produce. Estimates are that 300,000 man hours and 800,000 reichsmarks (about $200,000 US at that time) were spent on each Tiger I.

The Tiger's massive frontal armor enabled it to deflect Allied shells without harm, and

The best German medium tank of WWII was the Panther. Built in response to the fielding of the Soviet T34 medium tank, the Panther's powerful long-barreled 75mm gun and well-shaped armor made it a difficult target to destroy in combat. *National Archives*

its main gun could kill Allied tanks out to 2000yd. The Tiger's 88 sent its tungsten-cored 20lb armor-piercing shot on its way at 3,340 ft/sec, and that shot could penetrate more than 4in of armor at a 30deg slope at 2,400yd.

What made the Tiger such a fearsome opponent was that Shermans and Cromwells had to get within 700yd of it to get a shot through its side or rear armor. Attacking from the front was suicidal. It was stated in a British Army test report on firings of various Allied tank and antitank guns at a captured Tiger I that "in no instance was the frontal armor penetrated."

Despite its massive armor and its tank-killing 88mm gun, the Tiger was not invincible. The Tiger I of Capt. Michael Wittman, who was credited with the destruction of 138 tanks and assault guns and 132 antitank guns in fewer than two years of combat in Russia and France, was destroyed by a single British Sherman Firefly, which shot a number of rounds from its 17-pounder gun through the thinner rear armor of the tank.

Only 1,354 Tiger I tanks were built between late 1942 and August 1944 when it was replaced in production by the Tiger II. The Tiger II, also nicknamed the "King Tiger" by the Allies, featured a more powerful 88mm gun and had highly sloped armor protection.

Unfortunately, it was severely underpowered for its weight and had numerous engine and transmission problems. Only 485 Tiger II tanks were built before the end of WWII.

American factories, on the other hand, built almost 50,000 M4 Sherman tanks between 1942 and 1945, and the Soviets built an almost equal number of their famous T34 tanks. The Tigers were overwhelmed in combat by the more numerous Allied tanks backed by superior artillery and air support.

Of the very few Tiger tanks to survive WWII, all are currently on display in military museums in the United States, France, England, and the USSR. There are recent reports that a somewhat run-down Tiger I was recently sighted on an Army base in the former USSR. With the current financial problems in that part of the world, it may be possible that this vehicle would be offered for sale at some point in the future. Since the vehicle's condition is unknown and there are no spare parts to be had anywhere, it is very difficult to determine a possible price for such a historical vehicle. Nevertheless, certain very wealthy collectors would no doubt pay almost any price for a Tiger tank.

The British-built Churchill, like most other tanks of WWII, was continuously modified to keep pace with enemy weapons. First used by Canadian Army units during the attack on Dieppe in August 1942, the Churchill had both a small turret-mounted cannon and a hull-mounted cannon. Pictured is a Churchill tank that was destroyed on Dieppe Beach. *German Army*

German Panther Medium Tank

The second-most-feared German tank was the Panther, the most powerful medium tank built during WWII. Its design heavily influenced the types of tanks that both the British and American armies were building both at the end of the war and during the postwar era.

The Panther's rakish appearance and clean lines have inspired generations of modelers to build thousands upon thousands of models of the Panther tank in a wide variety of different scales.

What made the 45-ton Panther such a departure from other German tanks, as well as British and American tanks, was its very thick and well-sloped frontal armor. Unlike most other tanks of the time, which were basically square armored boxes, the Panther had well-sloped armor. German tank designers copied the sloped armor on the Soviet T34 because inclining the armor plate at more than 50 to 60deg effectively doubled its ballistic protection. For example, a 2in piece of steel armor plate placed at a 50 to 60deg angle would equal in protection a 4in steel armor plate in a vertical position. With this simple design feature, medium tanks could now have the armor protection of what only larger heavy tanks could carry in the past. Since steel armor has always been the heaviest element of most tanks, the less armor a tank featured, the lighter it was. Lighter vehicles are always preferred because they have better mobility, require less fuel, and can cross a larger number of bridges. It's only been in the last two decades with advancements in automotive performance that modern main battle tanks such as the M1A1 Abrams, which weighs more than the Tiger tanks of WWII, have been able to match the speed and cross-country mobility of some WWII-era light tanks.

German companies set out to build an even better medium tank than the T34. Unfortunately, with the war on the Eastern front growing in size and frenzy, Germany had to rush its new medium tank into production and combat before all the bugs were eliminated. Production of the Panther, began in November 1942, but it wasn't until 1943 that the Panther began appearing in combat in large numbers. Even so, the Germans built only

To improve the firepower of the Churchill, the British upgraded the vehicle with a 75mm cannon. Unfortunately, its turret ring didn't allow a larger gun to be fitted. As the 75mm gun was already obsolete against later-war German tanks, the Churchill was at a disadvantage in combat. Pictured is a Churchill with a 75mm gun on display at Aberdeen Proving Grounds, Maryland. *Michael Green*

6,600 Panther tanks of all types during WWII. Compared to approximately 50,000 Soviet T34 tanks and 50,000 American M4 Shermans built during the war, it didn't really make much difference if the Panther was the better tank. It was overwhelmed by numbers.

The Panther had a five-man crew: The vehicle commander, gunner, and loader sat in the turret and the driver and assistant driver sat in the front hull. The vehicle was powered by a Maybach twelve-cylinder water-cooled gas engine that could push the Panther to a top speed of 29mph with an operation range of 110 miles.

The Panther was armed with a very long (19ft 2-1/4in) 75mm high-velocity tank gun known as the Kwk42. This outstanding gun was fitted with a double-baffle muzzle brake and out-ranged every other medium-tank gun of its day. Only the British 17-pounder gun fitted Sherman Firefly variants and the

Army's M36 Tank Destroyer armed with a 90mm gun could equal the hitting power and performance of the Panther's 75mm gun. On the Russian front, the Panther was out-ranged by only a few of the Panther heavy tanks armed with 122mm guns.

With the end of WWII, the Panthers that survived were mostly cut up by scrap dealers. The French Army, which had lost its tank-building industry during the war, used at least fifty Panthers in conjunction with American-supplied Shermans for a few short years after the war until it could start fielding newer generations of postwar American tank designs. Most of the former-French Army Panthers were later shot up on firing ranges.

At least ten Panthers of various different models have survived in military museums. Only a single Panther tank, found in a British scrap yard in 1977, is owned by a private collector. Now fully restored, this vehicle is actually a postwar vehicle built under British Army supervision by German civilians with leftover parts from a German tank factory. At least ten of these postwar British Panthers were built for test and evaluation purposes. When the tests were completed, these vehicles were sold as scrap metal or shot up on British military firing ranges.

As with the German Tiger tank, a very rare and historical vehicle like the Panther tank would bring a very high price. If the single Panther tank in private hands was ever placed in the collector's marketplace, it would likely bring up to $200,000. On the flip side, there are no spare parts for this vehicle. If you wish to run it, you risk losing it. All Panther tanks were very prone to both transmission failures and engine fires. This would be strictly a display vehicle.

British A22 Mk. IV Churchill Tank

Generals always think that the next war will be just like the last one. When the Germans invaded Poland in September 1939 and started WWII, the British generals realized that they could quickly become involved in a European land conflict again. Since they believed that any future war in Europe would mirror World War I, with lots of trenches and shell-torn ground, they asked British industry to built a very large, heavily armored, infantry support tank that could cross wide trenches. This vehicle was to assist the infantry, so its speed was not required to be more than 10mph.

The British tank designers' first attempt to meet the Army's requirements was known as the A20. This vehicle proved to be too heavy

Like so many WWII-era American-made tanks, the M3 light tank was given or sold to friendly foreign countries around the world. In these foreign armies, many M3 light tanks survived in service until very recently. In Brazil, this line of M3 light tanks is waiting for the junk dealer or military vehicle collector to show up. *Jacques Littlefield*

and under-powered, and the project was canceled. In the meantime, the scope of the war in Europe had grown. France had fallen and a large part of the British Army and its equipment was lost in France. With a desperate need for more tanks to defend England from a feared German invasion, the British military asked designers to take another look at the canceled A20 tank design to see if it could be made somewhat smaller and lighter than the original design and rush it into production as soon as possible.

This scaled-down version of the A20 became the A22 infantry tank Mk. IV; the first-production models were ready in late 1940. Rushed into production, early models of this new tank, named the Churchill, were plagued by a host of problems. Altogether, 5,640 Churchills of different models were built during WWII, as well as several variations, including flame-throwers, armored recovery vehicles, and bridging vehicles.

Looking more like a World War I leftover than other tanks of WWII, the Churchill's long tracks ran at hull-top level on small-spring bogie assemblies, which allowed an incredible amount of space within the vehicle's hull. The Churchill had a five-man crew, very typical of most WWII medium tanks: The driver and an assistant driver sat in the front hull while the commander, gunner, and loader sat in the turret. There were escape hatches on the turret and hull for the crew.

Final production models of the Churchill were 24ft 5in long, 9ft wide, and 11ft 4in tall. The vehicle was powered by Bedford Twin six-cylinder gas engines which gave it a top speed of 15mph and an operational range of about 90 miles.

The heavy armor protection of the 40-ton Churchill made it a favorite among British tankers going up against German antitank weapons. While the Churchill's excellent cross-country mobility and thick armor made it one of the best British tanks to see action during WWII, its lack of firepower, when compared to that of German tanks, always left it at a disadvantage in combat. Early models of the Churchill had a small 40mm gun mounted in its turret and a 3in howitzer in the front hull. The British modified the vehicle with a 57mm gun in the turret and removed

the hull-mounted howitzer. By 1943, the Churchill was armed with a 75mm gun mounted in the turret. Unfortunately, this gun could not shoot through the well-sloped heavy armor of later-war German tanks such as the Panther or Tiger. Because the Churchill was too narrow to mount a bigger gun, the British were unable to mount their bigger antitank guns, as they did with the more adaptable American-built Sherman.

Besides seeing action with the British Army, a number of Churchills were also sent to the USSR. After WWII, the Churchill was supplied to a number of other countries. A few Churchills also saw action during the Korean War, where their hill-climbing ability proved very useful. Most Churchill tanks disappeared into scrap yards and target ranges by the late 1950s. There are 6–8 Churchills currently in private hands. Spare parts can be found with some effort, and the parts are not much more expensive than Sherman tank components. There is at least one individual in England who is making the hull fenders for the vehicle.

The Churchill is a great vehicle to drive. It has a very smooth-running engine and the transmission is fairly maintenance free. Unlike the Sherman or T34, the Churchill's steering controls are boosted and all hydraulically operated as are the brakes and throttle. As a

Belonging to a private collector, this M3 light tank is marked as a USMC tank. During the early stages of WWII, the USMC made extensive use of the M3 until it was replaced by the M4 Sherman medium tank. *Michael Green*

result, the Churchill is a fun and easy vehicle to drive. It has a very low first gear, making the vehicle a great hill climber.

Prices for a hulk can start at $20,000, with an operational vehicle typically selling for $60,000. A fully restored vehicle could cost as much as $80,000.

M3 Stuart Light Tank

From the late 1920s until the opening stages of WWII in September 1939, the Army began testing a wide variety of different light tanks, most of which never went beyond the prototype stage. It wasn't until 1939 that the Army decided to mass-produce a light tank known as the M2A4. Fitted with a 37mm cannon in a two-man turret, 375 M2A4s were built between 1939 and 1940. Due to combat reports from Europe, the Army decided to redesign the M2A4 light tank with heavier armor protection. In its new form, the vehicle now became the M3 light tank. Approved for production in July 1940, almost 14,000 different versions of the M3 light tank were built during the war years. Continuously improved as production went on, the M3 became the M3A1, M3A2, and the final model, the M3A3. The different models of the M3 series had a combination of riveted, welded, and cast-welded turrets. The M3 hulls were constructed of either riveted armor or welded armor plates.

The main armament of the M3 was the same 37mm cannon found in the earlier M2A4 light tank. Early M3 tanks were fitted with four .30cal machine guns, one alongside the 37mm gun in the turret and three firing forward from the front hull, two of the latter being fitted in the side hull compartments of the vehicle. These were later removed since they were so inaccurate. Retained was the .30cal mounted in the front hull and operated by the vehicle's assistant driver.

Many of the early-production M3s were supplied to the British forces fighting Rommel's Afrikakorps in the deserts of North Africa. The British Army's official name for the M3 was the General Stuart, but most British tankers called it the "Honey" because

The M3 was replaced by the M5 light tank, which was powered by two Cadillac gas engines, coupled to an automatic transmission. Pictured is an M5 series light tank during a training exercise in the United States. *National Archives*

The M3 light tank was armed with a 37mm cannon and several machine guns. This WWII-era Army photo clearly shows the rivet construction of the M3 hull. In combat, rivets that were hit by enemy rounds tended to fly into the crew compartment of the M3, causing serious wounds to the crew members. *National Archives*

of its superior mechanical reliability compared to British tanks of the period.

The M3 series of light tanks had a four-man crew. The vehicle itself was 14ft 10in long, 7ft 4in wide, and 7ft 6in tall. Later models were a little shorter because no cupola was fitted on the turret. Fully loaded, the M3 series weighed about 14 tons. Most vehicles were powered by a radial, air-cooled, aircraft-type gas engine which provided a top speed of 35mph and an operational range of about 70 miles. The engine had 250hp at 2,400rpm. About 500 of the M3 series of light tanks were fitted with diesel engines.

While the vehicle proved to be very fast and reliable, combat experience quickly showed that the M3 was undergunned and underarmored when compared to German tanks. It was declared obsolete in Army service in July 1943, but continued in service with other Allied armies until the end of WWII and beyond.

After WWII, many M3 tanks were given or sold to Latin American countries, including Mexico and Brazil. Both countries had close to 200 vehicles in their inventories. Mexico was still using its M3's until the late 1970s, and Brazil rebuilt and rearmed some of its old M3s with 90mm lightweight cannons.

Having continued in service for so many years in so many different countries, a number of M3's have found their way into collectors' hands. The vehicle is popular among some collectors since it is a very fast and maneuverable vehicle despite it's radial engine and clutch. The interior is somewhat cramped, but the excellent visibility offered from the driver's and assistant driver's position is much better than most other tanks. A serious drawback to having a radial-engine-powered tank, is that very few people have any experience in working on them.

An M3 series hulk can bring about $20,000, an operational vehicle $35,000, and a fully restored vehicle at least $50,000. Fortunately for collectors, automotive parts are readily available for the M3 light tank. Other components like turret baskets and ammo racks are a little harder to find. Currently, there are about 20 M3 series light tanks in private hands.

The M5 light tank was still fitted with the same 37mm cannon as found on the M3 light tank. This cannon was completely obsolete by WWII standards and caused the M5 light tank to generally be confined to secondary roles. The biggest visible difference between the M3 and M5 series light tanks was the sloping front hull plate of the M5. *National Archives*

M5 Light Tank

Because of the growing shortage of aircraft-type radial gas engines for its tank fleet, the Army began investigating other types of engines for both its light and medium tanks. The Cadillac Division of GM suggested that twin Cadillac gas car engines be installed into the M3 light tanks. This idea resulted in a single prototype vehicle that proved so successful in tests that the Army approved production of this new vehicle and standardized it as the M5 light tank in February 1942. The first-production M5 was finished in March 1942 by Cadillac. Massey-Harris and American Car and Foundry also built M5 light tanks during WWII.

Coupled to the twin Cadillac engines in the M5 were two Cadillac hydraulic automatic transmissions which brought the top speed of the vehicle to almost 40mph. Operational range was approximately 160 miles. Improvements to the armor increased the vehicle's weight approximately two tons over that of the earlier M3. Weighing almost 16 tons, the M5's dimensions were very similar to those of the earlier M3: 14ft 7in long, 7ft 4in wide, and 7ft 10in high.

The small size of the M5 light tank and its relatively simple construction makes it a popular tank among collectors. The M5 tank pictured here belongs to Fred Ropkey. *Fred Ropkey*

To improve its chances of hitting a target in combat, the M5 had a power traverse system plus a gyrostabilizer for firing while moving. A new gun mounting featured a better telescope to aim the vehicle's 37mm main gun. Extra periscopes were also added to the turret to give the crew better visibility with the hatches closed.

Other changes incorporated into the M5 and an improved model known as the M5A1 included a new turret with a bulge at the rear for radio equipment and larger hatches for the driver and assistant driver. The M5A1 was a little bigger than the M5: 15ft 10-1/2in long, 7ft 6in wide, and 7ft 10-1/2in tall. At its thickest point, the armor on the M5A1 was only 2-1/2in. The biggest visual difference between the M5 and M5A1 was the fitting of sheet-metal fairings on either side of the M5A1 turret, which were used to protect the .50cal machine gun normally mounted on top of the M5A1 turret when it was in its stowed position.

While the M5 and M5A1 were a big improvement over the original M3 light tanks, they were still badly underarmored and undergunned against German tanks and anti-tank weapons.

Only 8,884 M5 and M5A1 light tanks were built before the Army declared them obsolete in July 1944. They did continue to see limited service until the end of WWII but were quickly replaced in Europe during the winter of 1944 by the M24, armed with a 75mm gun.

Like the earlier M3 light tank series, the M5 and M5A1 light tanks were given or sold to friendly governments around the world after the war ended in 1945. Many Third World countries continued to use the M5 series until very recently. As these Third World armies acquired newer vehicles, the M5s were sold as scrap or returned to the US government for disposal, but close to 80 M5s were acquired by private collectors.

Because of its compact size and light weight the M5 series light tanks are the perfect choice for a collector who has to have a WWII tank, but doesn't have much storage room. Another plus is the vehicle's easy-to-work-on, twin engines. Parts are also readily available for the vehicle. Since the M5 series light tanks used Cadillac car engines, even car restoration dealers have many engine components that can be used to rebuild the tank's engines.

Compared to the M3 light tank series, the M5 series has better riding characteristics and its engines make less noise than the M3's radial engine. Because almost every mechanic is familiar with the old Cadillac engines used to power the M5, it won't be hard for a collector to find help when he needs it.

In 1944, the M24 light tank reached Europe and began to replace the obsolete M3 and M5 light tanks still in service. Mounting a 75mm cannon, the M24 was a big improvement over the 37mm gun mounted in the earlier light tanks. The vehicle shown is on display at Fort Hood, Texas. *Bill Rosenmund*

Prices for M5 series light tanks start at $15,000 for a hulk, $35,000 for an operational vehicle, and close to $50,000 or more for a fully restored model.

M24 Chaffee Light Tank

Very early in WWII, the Army realized that its fleet of M3 and M5 series of light tanks was completely useless against German tanks and antitank guns. In early 1943, Cadillac began work on a new light tank prototype known as the T24. The prototype featured two rear-mounted, water-cooled Cadillac V-8 engines and a hydraulic transmission. Unlike the M3 and M5 series, which had the older generation, vertical volute-spring suspension system, the T24 prototype had a torsion-bar suspension system based on that of the high-speed M18 Hellcat tank destroyer. To upgrade the firepower of the new tank, a lightweight 75mm gun developed for the B-25 medium bomber was installed. It fired the same ammunition as the M4 Sherman's 75mm gun. With a short barrel and low muzzle velocity, this modified aircraft cannon

Belonging to a private collector, this former-French Army M24 light tank is slowly being restored to fully operational condition. Because of its small size and weight compared to that of larger tanks, the M24 light tank is very popular among armor vehicle collectors. *Michael Green*

could not take on heavily armored German tanks, but since it was designed as a reconnaissance and infantry support vehicle, this was not considered a handicap. Armor was no more than 1in thick. Production began in April 1944 and the designation was changed to Light Tank M24. The Army named it the Chaffee in honor of Gen. Adna R. Chaffee, considered the Father of the United States Armed Forces. Chaffee had died in late 1941 without seeing action in WWII.

Almost 5,000 M24s were built during WWII by both Cadillac and Massey-Harris. The first M24s reached Western Europe and the Army in late 1944, just in time to see action during the Battle of the Bulge in December 1944.

In addition to its 75mm gun, the M24 was armed with three machine guns, a bow-mounted .30cal in the front hull, another .30cal fitted to fire alongside the main gun, and a .50cal mounted on the roof of the turret for antiaircraft protection and as a ground fire weapon. The M24 had a five-man crew: The vehicle commander, gunner, and loader sat in the turret, while the driver and assistant driver sat in the front hull. The vehicle's running gear consisted of five sets of paired road wheels and three return rollers on each side of the hull. The M24 had front-mounted drive sprockets with rear-mounted idler wheels.

The M24's twin V-8 Cadillac engines gave it a top speed of 34mph and an operational range of about 100 miles (very typical of gas-powered tanks of the period).

After WWII, the M24 became the Army's standard light tank. With the outbreak of the Korean War in June 1950, the M24 was the first American tank sent to Korea. Unable to stand up to the North Korean T34/85 tanks (supplied by the USSR), however, the M24 was quickly replaced by M4 Shermans armed with 76mm guns and M26 and M46 tanks armed with 90mm guns. Replaced in American military service by the M41 light tank in the mid-1950s, the M24 continued to serve in many other armies around the world. Even today, Norway has a small fleet of upgraded M24 tanks armed with low-pressure 90mm guns and laser range finders.

The largest user of M24s outside of the United States was France. Having received more than 1,000 M24s from the United States, French military forces made widespread use of the vehicle during their war in Indochina. After the French military forces left Indochina during 1955, those remaining M24 tanks were passed onto the newly formed Army of the Republic of Vietnam. The US government also supplied an additional number of M24 tanks from their inventory. Eventually, the M24s in Vietnamese service were replaced by American-supplied M41 light tanks. The South Vietnamese Air Force did keep a few M24s for airport security and anti-coup duties. These vehicles were still in service at the end of the Vietnam War when North Vietnamese Army (NVA) units overran Saigon.

Due to its smaller size and weight when compared to most other main battle tanks, the M24 is fairly popular among collectors. Because it had a long service life in foreign armies, a number of companies continued to make replacement parts. There are about seven M24s now in private hands. Prices for M24 hulks start at approximately $25,000. An operational M24 can cost $45,000. For a fully restored example, the price can reach as high as $85,000.

Compared to the M3 and M5 series light tank the M24 is fairly roomy. The M24 also has no turret basket. This means you can allow visitors to ride inside the vehicle, without fear that somebody will catch a foot or arm in between the turret basket and hull when the turret is turned. The M24 is an easier vehicle to drive than the M3 and M5 light tank series and also provides a smoother ride.

In addition to its main armament of a 75mm cannon, the M24 was also armed with three machine guns. One .50cal machine gun was mounted on the top of the turret. There was also a hull-mounted .30cal machine gun operated by the assistant driver and another .30cal machine gun fitted to fire alongside the main gun. *US Army*

To replace the M24 light tank, the Army developed a new light tank known as the M41. First built in 1951, the M41 light tank was armed with a 76mm cannon and two machine guns. Shown in Europe during the 1950s, a column of M41s are passing through a small town during a training exercise. *US Army*

On the flip side, M24 parts seem to be harder to find than other WWII American tank parts. The parts are also much more expensive to buy when you can find them.

Because the M24 is wider and heavier than the M3 and M5 light tank series, they are a little harder to move on the highway and may require a heavy-duty trailer. In contrast, the M3 and M5s can be towed around to collector events on a simple tilt-bed trailer.

M41 Walker Bulldog Light Tank

Shortly after the end of WWII, the Army began work on a new light tank that eventually became known as the M41. The first-production model was built in 1951 at the government-owned Cleveland Tank Plant which was run at the time by the Cadillac Car Division of GM.

Originally named Little Bulldog by the Army, the M41 was later dubbed the Walker Bulldog after Gen. Walton W. Walker, who was killed in a jeep accident during the Korean War.

Armed with a 76mm cannon and two machine guns, the M41 had a crew of four, weighed about 25 tons, and had a top speed of about 45mph.

Built too late to see combat during the Korean War, the M41 was designed as a reconnaissance vehicle. Its job was to slip through enemy lines, locate or engage strategic targets, and hurry back to safety before any serious enemy resistance could be formed.

Because it had to be fast and nimble for its scouting role, the M41 had very thin armor, resistant only against small arms fire and artillery fragments. Due to its small size, space in the M41 was very cramped. The driver, who sat at the front of the vehicle on the left side, lived in mortal terror of the turret, which stuck out over him. If the driver had his head out of the hatch when the turret was turned without his knowledge, he could easily have his neck broken.

The M41 was powered by a Continental or Lycoming six-cylinder, air-cooled, supercharged gas engine, which produced 500hp at 2,800rpm. It had an operational range of no more than 100 miles, typical of other gas-powered American tanks of the time. Later, the M41 was fitted with a modified engine with a fuel-injection system that slightly boosted its operational range.

The M41's engine was very noisy. In low gear, it would scream so loud that they could be heard hundreds of yards away. In other gears, the engine produced a constantly loud whining noise, and the exposed muffler covers on the rear hull fenders got so hot that they glowed cherry-red in the dark. American tank crews, however, overlooked these design flaws and thought the M41 was very dependable. They also liked the vehicle's high speed and responsive handling, which, combined with its small size, made it easy to conceal. The M41 was tall at 10ft 1in, but it was only 19ft 1in long and 10ft 6in wide. In comparison, the 10ft 2in-tall M48 Patton was more than 22ft 7in long and 11ft 11in wide.

A total of 5,500 M41 light tanks were built between 1951 and 1959. Replaced in the early 1960s by newer vehicles in the Army, most were given or sold to foreign armies. Some updated M41s still serve in various parts of the world. Pictured is an Army M41 on a firing range. Notice the 76mm rounds on the ground. *US Army*

Like all tanks, the M41 was constantly improved during its service life and came in numerous variations. Altogether, 5,500 M41s were built between 1951 and 1959.

The M41 was phased out of US Army service in the late 1960s in favor of the new M551 Sheridan light tank. The Army considered the 76mm gun on the M41 to be inadequate against newer Soviet tanks such as the T54 and T55. The M41 was given or sold to almost thirty other countries. Being easy to operate and maintain, it proved to be popular.

Among the largest users of American-supplied M41 tanks was the Army of the Republic of Vietnam, which received its first of almost 300 M41 tanks in 1965. During the Vietnam War, the South Vietnamese successfully used their M41s to destroy NVA T54 and

PT76 tanks in combat. Unfortunately, the biggest threat to most American and South Vietnamese tanks during the Vietnam War were land mines which ripped apart the M41's thin hull armor.

M41 tanks also saw combat in 1961 during the CIA-sponsored Bay of Pigs invasion of Cuba. The CIA supplied the American-trained Cuban invasion force with five M41 tanks. No match against the Soviet-supplied tanks and doomed to fail, the M41s were destroyed by their crews before they surrendered to Castro's soldiers.

While a number of M41s are available on the collectors' market, some countries continue to use them, rather than purchase new, more expensive tanks. Brazil, Denmark, and Spain have modernized their fleets of M41s with new engines and improved fire-control systems. Spain went a step further and developed a prototype M41 into an antitank missile-equipped tank destroyer, replacing the turret with a missile launching system that fires either American TOW or French HOT antitank missiles.

The last American use of the M41 was by the US Navy. Removing the turret and mounting a small platform carrying a number of high-intensity lights upon it, the Navy used a few M41s as remote-controlled target tanks to help them test its air-to-ground missiles. In this configuration, the M41 became known as the QM41. No longer in service, one remaining example of this strange modification is in storage at the Patton Armor Museum.

Currently, there are about twelve M41s in private hands. Prices for hulks start at $25,000 and run up to $55,000 for an operational vehicle. A fully restored vehicle could run between $75,000 to $90,000.

The M41 is an impressive looking tank.

Belonging to a private collector, this M41 is missing its 76mm main gun. Because of its size and weight, the M41 is popular among collectors. *Michael Green*

However, the vehicle's width and weight mandates that a special permit is needed to move the vehicle by public roads, since it will overhang the standard commercial trailer.

Because the M41 is a postwar vehicle and still in the inventory of some armies, parts are available, but they tend to be fairly expensive. As an example, a new stock rebuilt C1 radial engine for a WWII Sherman costs between $900 and $2,000. In contrast, the six-cylinder engine on the M41 typically costs $3,500 and at least another $2,000 for the transmission.

M26 Pershing Medium Tank

Throughout WWII, the various branches of the Army involved in tank design could not agree on the type of vehicle needed to replace the M4 Sherman. While the Army had begun work on a number of prototype medium and heavy tanks as early as 1942, nothing ever came of them. It wasn't until after the D-day invasion of Europe on June 6, 1944, that the Army began to realize just how undergunned and underarmored the Sherman was against later-war German tanks. Belatedly, the Army hurried into production a vehicle known as the T26E2 medium tank, armed with a 90mm gun. Redesignated as a heavy tank in June 1944, a handful were rushed to Europe during the closing days of WWII and saw limited combat against German tanks. The Army called the T26E2 a heavy tank, but at 41 tons, it was more comparable to the 45-ton Panther medium tank than to the 60-ton Tiger heavy tank .

In March 1945, the T26E2 became the M26 Pershing tank.

In the years following WWII, almost 2,500 M26s were built. The M26 saw extensive combat during the Korean War. At the same time, the Army began to improve the M26 with a new engine and transmission, leading to its redesignation as the M46 Patton tank.

The M26 was powered by a modified Ford GAA engine, known as the GAF. With its 500hp, the Ford engine was very successful in pushing the 35-ton Sherman around, but it was not powerful enough for the 41-ton M26 tank. In the Korean War, the M4A3 Sherman was preferred over the M26 because it could more easily climb over the very mountainous Korean terrain.

To deal with later-war German heavy tanks such as the Tiger, the Army deployed the M26 Pershing at the end of WWII. While the vehicle saw limited combat action against German tanks, it was widely used during the Korean War. The USMC M26 pictured has just run over a land mine, which has broken its track. *USMC*

With about 4in of cast-steel armor on its front hull and 4.5in on the front turret gun mantle, the M26 was much better armored than the Sherman. Still, the Army thought that the armor could have been better designed and began making improvements for later American tank designs.

The M26 tank had a five-man crew: three sitting in the turret and two in the front hull. It rode on a torsion-bar suspension system and was 22ft 4in long, 11ft 6in wide, and 9ft 1in high. The Ford GAF gas engine could push the vehicle up to a top speed of 30mph, with an operational range of approximately 110 miles.

Most M26 tanks were rebuilt into M46 tanks during and after the Korean War. A few saw service with the French, Greek, and Turkish armies for a number of years. Currently, there are only two M26 tanks in collectors' hands.

The two M26 hulks now in collectors' hands could bring up to $20,000 because of their rarity. An operational vehicle could fetch up to $65,000 and a fully restored example could range between $75,000 to $100,000.

Because of the weight and size of the M26 tank, and other American-built postwar medium tanks like the M47, M48, and M60 series, the collector who wishes to own such vehicles must face the fact that he will almost never be able to move them off his property once they have arrived. The only reason for owning such vehicles is their historical value. To keep any AFV over 40 tons in running condition requires the attention of more than just

The M26 Pershing was armed with a 90mm cannon adapted from an antiaircraft gun. It had a five-man crew and was powered by a 500hp Ford gas engine. *US Army*

one person. In their military life, all these tanks had squads of mechanics with special tools to look after them. Only the most well-to-do collectors can afford the men and equipment to keep heavy AFVs running.

M47 Patton Medium Tank

When the Korean War broke out in 1950, the Army found itself seriously short of modern tanks. Most of the Korean War was fought with the M4 Sherman and the M26 Pershing—both of which were considered obsolete by the Army when compared to newer postwar Soviet tanks of the time.

The most modern US tank in use during the Korean War was the M46 medium tank, which was an upgraded M26 Pershing with a new engine and transmission. Externally, M26 and M46 looked very similar except for a different type of 90mm gun and a modified rear engine deck on the M46. The Army officially nicknamed all main battle tanks from the M46 medium tank through the later M47

and M48 series the Patton tanks in honor of Gen. George Patton of WWII fame.

Even though the M46 tank was in full production at the beginning of the Korean War, there were not enough to satisfy South Korean military requirements. The Army considered many features of the M46 obsolete and did not want to start a new production line for it, instead taking the new turret of a prototype tank known as the T42 and mounting it on the M46 hull. Although armed with the same 90mm gun as found in the M46 tank, the new turret had a better ballistic shape and was fitted with an advanced stereoscopic range finder. The Army called its new tank the M47. Production began in June 1951 and ended in November 1953, with 8,576 units built.

Rushed into production, early tests showed that there were numerous problems with the tank's turret and fire-control system. A few M47s were sent to Korea in the closing

The M47 Patton medium tank was armed with a 90mm cannon and three machine guns. A total 8,676 M47s were produced. Too late to see action in the Korean War, the M47 had several shortcomings, which led to its fairly quick replacement by the M48 Patton tank. *US Army*

The most distinctly visible feature on the M47 Patton tank was the overhanging bustle at the rear of the turret. A light steel storage box was fitted to the rear of this bustle. These M47 tanks are on an Army firing range. *US Army*

days of the Korean War, but none saw combat action. Most M47 tanks were instead shipped to Army units in West Germany.

Unhappy with the numerous problems in fielding the M47, the Army had already begun work on its replacement even as it was being fielded. As a result, the M47 tank saw only limited service with American tank units before the M48 Patton took its place.

As the American military had done during WWII with various types of tanks it didn't consider up-to-par, it gave them in large numbers to its allies. With the forming of the North Atlantic Treaty Organization (NATO) in the late 1950s, numerous Western European armies, especially those of France, Italy, and West Germany, were either given or bought from the United States large numbers of surplus M47 tanks. Other countries that have used the M47 include Belgium, Greece, Brazil, Saudi Arabia, Taiwan, Turkey, Yugoslavia, Austria, Iran, and Spain.

The M47 saw its first combat in 1956 with a French tank unit during the British-French at-tack on Port Said, Egypt. In 1965, Pakistan used the almost 400 M47s it had received from the United States against India during a month-long border dispute. During the 1967 Six Day War, M47s of the Jordanian Army saw heavy action against Israeli Sherman tanks. A few M47s also saw combat during the very early days of the still ongoing civil war in Ethiopia.

The most visible M47 tanks are the ones belonging to the Spanish Army because they are often rented to US and European movie companies, typically portraying German Tigers. Movies featuring the M47 include *Patton* and *Battle of the Bulge*.

With a weight of 55 tons, the M47 was considered a medium tank by the Army. It had a five-man crew: three sitting in the turret and two in the front hull. As with all American tanks of the period, the M47 was powered by a Continental AV-1790-5A gas engine. This engine, coupled to a CD-85 cross-drive transmission, would form the basic power of American tanks for the next three decades.

Belonging to a private collector, this M47 tank is being restored to operational condition. *Michael Green*

The M47 could reach 37mph and had a top operational range of about 100 miles.

In addition to the 90mm main gun, the M47 was armed with two .30cal and one .50cal machine gun mounted on top of its turret.

There are at least 20 or more M47s now in private hands. Prices for a hulk start at $20,000, with an operational vehicle costing about $30,000. A fully restored M47 may go for $50,000.

Owning and operating an M47 tank is not an easy thing to do. Because of the size and weight of the vehicle it is very difficult to work on without specialized lifting equipment. Even raising the armored access doors to the engine compartment requires two strong men. Transporting the M47 by high-

way would require both the renting of a specialized heavy-duty low-boy trailer (very expensive) and obtaining special police permits for moving an oversized load.

Other than being a heavy tank armed with a 90mm gun, there is little advantage to owning something like an M47 medium tank compared to a light tank like the M41. However, if you must have one for your collection. There are some advantages. Powerpacks and engines are available at very reasonable prices. Plus, the engines are fairly easy to work on because there is no fuel-injection system fitted. The vehicle also has a cross-drive transmission, so they are very easy to drive. A big plus for collectors who wish to show somebody else how to drive a tank, is the fact that the vehicle has dual driving controls. A fea-

Used as a training aid for Fort Ord, California, this very early-model T54 tank was captured by the Is-raeli Army from the Egyptian Army and later given to the US Army for study. *Michael Green*

The diesel engines that powered the T54 and T55 tanks was mounted transversely at the rear of the hull. Access to the engine for maintenance or repair was very difficult. These two American soldiers are trying to figure out the best way to fix the engine on this early-model T54. *Michael Green*

ture it shares with the American WWII light tanks M3, M5, and M24.

Soviet T54 and T55 Medium Tanks

The T54 series of tanks first appeared in Soviet military service in 1949. The T54 was a development of an earlier tank known as the T44, which itself was a development of the T34 tank of WWII. The Soviets continuously improved and modified the T54 tank until sufficient changes had been made, and then redesignated it as the T55. The T55 was first seen in Soviet service in 1958. It incorporated all the improvements of the fully developed T54 series but was not radically different in design or appearance. The T55 was also continuously improved by the Soviets until it evolved into the T62.

More T54s and T55s were built in the years since WWII than any other tank. It is estimated that almost 50,000 rolled off the factory floor since 1949. The USSR stopped production of the T55 in 1979, but production continued in Czechoslovakia and Poland until very recently and China still builds a copy of the T55 known as the Type 62. Iraq bought many Type 62s, but they fared very poorly against the more modern weapons used by the United States and its various Allies during Operation Desert Storm.

In general, Soviet tank development has always stressed quantity of vehicles produced and has concentrated on smaller, light, simpler vehicles that cost less to build, whereas the United States and other Western countries have spent more time and money on fewer larger, more complicated tanks. Instead of building new tanks, the Soviets preferred to upgrade older tanks, deploying them as quickly as possible and in as large a number as possible.

The Soviets have always believed in building lighter tanks, both because weight equals more cost for comparable agility and due to the limitations of their existing tank engines and transmissions. While the T54/55s weighed about 40 tons, the American M48 and M60 each weighed more than 55 tons. The Army's current main battle tank, the M1A1 Abrams, tops out at almost 70 tons combat loaded.

The T54/55 hull consisted entirely of welded-steel armor. The driver sat at the front left of the hull, and the vehicle commander, gunner, and loader sat in a half-egg-shaped turret. Both the vehicle commander and loader had one-piece hatch covers. The 100mm main gun mounted in the middle of the T54/55 turret was developed from an older naval gun. The T54 could carry thirty-four main gun rounds, and the T55 could carry forty-three. In comparison, the American M60 tank can carry sixty rounds. There was also a technical problem with the cramped turret: With less room in which to move about or to use its very crude fire-control equipment, the crew was unable to fire as quickly or as accurately

as the crews of Western tanks.

Soviet tank turrets could not be turned nearly as quickly or as precisely as Western tank turrets, enabling Western tanks to engage flank targets sooner and track moving targets better. Furthermore, most T54/55s were fitted with infrared night-vision devices that were inferior to the much more advanced thermal imagining devices fitted to most Western tanks since the 1980s.

Some of the last-production run T55s were upgraded with laser range finders, add-on armor, smoke grenade launchers, and track skirts to protect the vehicle's suspension system. The Czechs improved some of their T55s with a cross-wind sensor and a warning device that would alert the crew when the tank was being targeted by a laser aiming device.

The engines of the T54/55s were also improved over the years. The standard engine for a T55 was a water-cooled, twelve-cylinder diesel engine producing 580hp at 2,000rpm, giving the tank a top speed of about 30mph

On display at an Army base is this Iraqi T69 II main battle tank. Captured during Operation Desert Storm, the T69 is a Chinese-made copy of the Soviet T54 tank. *Richard Bryd*

Like the T34 tank, the T54 and T55 were widely exported around the world. However, combat experience has shown the vehicle to be poorly designed and unsuccessful in combat against Western-designed tanks. The vehicle pictured is a Finnish Army T55 tank during a training exercise. *Finnish Army*

and an operational range of approximately 250 miles. The engine itself was mounted sideways in the rear hull and was provided with an electric starter for normal operation. There was a compressed-air system for cold weather starting. The transmission was also located in the rear hull.

Both the T54 and T55 rode on a torsion-bar suspension system consisting of five road wheels per side. The idlers were at the front of the hull and the drive sprockets were at the rear. Only the first and fifth road wheels were fitted with hydraulic shock absorbers.

The T54/55s could be fitted with a snorkel for deep-fording operations across streams and rivers. The equipment took about 30min to assemble, but could be jettisoned immediately upon leaving the water.

In addition to the 100mm main gun, the T54/55s all mounted a coaxial 7.62mm machine gun fitted to fire alongside the main gun. Most T54s had a turret-mounted 12.7mm antiaircraft machine gun fitted to the loader's position, but this was deleted from most T55s.

The T54/55 has been replaced by newer tanks in the former Warsaw Pact countries, and is considered obsolete by most armies. Due to the various arms reduction treaties now in effect, most surviving T54/55 tanks will be scrapped in large numbers in the next few years. Also, because many former Warsaw Pact countries are in dire financial straits and no longer need large numbers of older-generation AFVs, almost everything is for sale.

An operational T54/55 can be had for approximately $20,000 on today's market. However, to ship a T54/55 from England or Europe to the United States may cost you as much as the price of the vehicle itself. On the positive side, the T54/55s are fairly easy to drive and maintain. They are not as comfortable to drive as postwar American tanks. But, as most collectors will not drive their tanks with the hatches closed, the tanks are bearable. Parts are easier to find than those for the older T34 tanks from WWII and can be had for reasonable prices.

Currently there are at least twenty T54/55 tanks in private hands. For the collector who wishes to have a complete, fully restored vehicle, the price goes up to about $30,000.

US M48 Patton Medium Tank

The best known American tank of the post-war-era is the M48 medium tank. First entering service with the Army in 1953, almost 12,000 various models were built between 1953 and 1959 by Chrysler, GM, and Ford Motor Co.

Designed to replace the problem-plagued M47 medium tank in Army service, the M48 tank hull and turret were made of thick cast-steel armor. The turret was elliptical shaped and offered a higher level of protection than that found on earlier turrets. The M48 hull had also been designed to be as rounded as possible to deflect the blast when running over land mines. The most visible part of the hull, the front or "glacis" in military terms, had a very distinctive boat-shaped bow to it.

The driver sat in the front hull and had a single-piece hatch cover fitted with three periscopes. The M48 was the first American medium tank to have a single driver. The M48 turret contained the vehicle commander, loader, and gunner. The vehicle commander had a separate, much smaller turret fitted to the top of the main turret, known as a "cupola." The cupola was traversed by hand and mounted a .50cal machine gun and carried vision blocks and a sight for the machine gun.

Almost half of the 12,000 M48 tanks built ended up in foreign armies. It was in the service of Pakistan's Army that the M48 first saw combat in 1965 during a border dispute with India. In a month-long conflict, Pakistani M47 and M48 tanks engaged in combat with Indian Army Centurion and Sherman tanks. Pakistani crews found the M47 and M48 fire-control systems too complicated for use in the field. Between the low level of tank crew training and poor tactical handling, the Pakistanis lost almost 500 tanks and other AFVs.

In American military service, the M48 saw its first and last combat action during the Vietnam War. The first M48s arrived with the USMC in South Vietnam in 1965. American military leaders had not envisioned using tanks in South Vietnam, but they eventually changed their minds, and M48s saw action al-

The first-production M48 medium tank rolled off the factory floor in July 1952, armed with the same 90mm gun as found on the M47 medium tank. The total production run of all models of the M48 series was 11,703 vehicles. This very early-model M48 is on display at Fort Hood, Texas. *Bill Rosenmund*

Later models of the M48 series were upgraded with both a 105mm gun and a diesel engine. In US military service, this vehicle was known as the M48A5. Pictured is a former California National Guard M48A5 during a training exercise. No longer in Army service, the M48A5 has been given or sold to several friendly governments. *Michael Green*

The T62 was developed from the earlier T54/55 series of Soviet tanks. Entering production in 1961, almost 20,000 were built before production ended in 1975. T62s were also built for export in Czechoslovakia between 1973 and 1978. North Korea also built it own version of the T62 tank. *Michael Green*

most everywhere in South Vietnam and Cambodia.

While the original M48 tank was powered by the same short-range gas engine found in the M47, by the early 1960s, the M48 had been re-powered with a diesel engine that increased its operational range from fewer than 100 miles to almost 300 miles. In this new configuration, the M48 became the M48A3. Still armed with a 90mm gun, the M48A3 became the mainstay of the Army, USMC, and, much later, the Army of the Republic of Vietnam. During the last stages of the war, M48A3 tanks engaged in combat with NVA (Soviet- and Chinese-supplied) tanks, doing very well until overrun by sheer numbers.

After the Vietnam War, the M48A3 tanks were up-gunned, along with any older versions of the M48 series, with the 105mm gun. In this configuration, the M48A3 became the M48A5 tank. The M48A5 tank was primarily used by Reserve and National Guard units until the late 1980s, when they were withdrawn from service. In this final version, the cupola was replaced with an Israeli-designed low-profile cupola, mounting a 7.62mm machine gun. This cupola was very similar to that found on the very first models of the M48

tank series. The Israelis adopted this new design because they thought the older cupola raised the height of the vehicle too much and because it was too small and cramped to be used by the tank commander.

Upgraded M48 tanks equipped with the 105mm gun and a diesel engine are still in widespread use around the world. Germany has recently withdrawn its fleet of M48s, but

The turret and hull of the M48 were much better shaped ballistically than those on the earlier M47 tank. The M48's armored hull was somewhat boat-shaped with a very pointed bow, which helped deflect mine blasts. *Michael Green*

other countries, including Greece, Turkey, Spain, Norway, and South Korea, show signs of using the M48 for a long time.

At the present time there are at least eight M48s in collectors' hands. Prices for a hulk start at $25,000, with an operational model going for at least $60,000. A fully restored vehicle may bring up to $80,000.

The M48 has many of the same good and bad characteristics as the M47. Since the M48 is a newer tank, the steering controls are a little bit better. Unfortunately, there is only a single driver's position in the front hull. Making it very difficult for a collector to teach somebody else how to drive his vehicle. Most collectors without prior tank driving experience must learn to handle their vehicles through trial and error. This should only be done with the help of others who can assist the driver in making the experience a safe one.

Soviet T62 Medium Tank

The most modern Soviet tank available on the current collectors' market is the 40-ton T62 medium tank. First seen in 1961 and using many components of existing vehicles, the T62 was basically an improved T55 tank with a bigger gun.

The T62 had a 580hp, V-12, water-cooled diesel engine. The tank also shared the snorkeling and smoke screen-generating capabilities of the T54/55 series. Most models had the same infrared night sight and driving equipment and the same fire-control equipment as the T54/55. Some T62s, however, received a passive night-sight system.

The most significant improvement over the T54/55 tanks, however, was the 115mm smoothbore main gun that fired a high-velocity, armor-piercing, fin-stabilized, discarding sabot (HVAPFSDS) round with a muzzle velocity of 1,615m per second. The penetrator flew in a very flat trajectory, making it extremely accurate.

The 115mm smoothbore main gun had a longer and thinner tube than the 100mm gun of the T54/55. Its bore evacuator was about

Two very early-model M60 tanks with rounded turrets are stopped in a small German town during a training exercise. *US Army*

To improve the ballistic protection of the M60 turret, a more needle-nosed turret was developed. In its new version, the vehicle became the M60A1. This

M60A1 of the 8th Infantry Division is parked in a West German forest in the winter of 1974. *US Army*

two-thirds of the way up the gun tube from the turret. There was also a 7.62mm coaxial machine gun.

A gunner's infrared searchlight was mounted on the right, above the main gun, and a smaller infrared searchlight was mounted on the commander's cupola. The driver's hatch was in front of the turret on the left side of the flat, low-silhouetted hull.

The T62 also had an automatic shell ejector system activated by the recoil of the main gun. Spent casings were ejected through a port in the rear of the turret.

The T62 medium tank had a fully tracked, five-road-wheeled chassis. The chassis had close spaces between the third, fourth, and fifth road wheels. The drive sprocket was at the rear and the idler was at the front; there were no track return rollers. The rounded turret, mounted over the third road wheel, was more smoothly cast and more nearly egg-

shaped than that of the T54/55 series. The commander's cupola on the left was cast with the turret. The loader's hatch on the right was also farther forward.

While the T62 was a big improvement over the T54/55 series, it still suffered from many of the same shortcomings: a cramped crew compartment, thin armor, crude gun control equipment (on most models), limited depression of the main gun, and vulnerable fuel and ammunition storage areas. The automatic spent-cartridge ejection system could cause dangerous accumulations of carbon monoxide, as well as possible physical injury to the crew from cartridge cases projected against the edge of a poorly aligned ejection port and rebounding into the crew compartment.

By the early 1970s, the T62 was showing its age when compared to newer and improved American and NATO tanks. Exported in large numbers to the various Arab nations fighting

Israel, the T62 tank did not perform very well in the hands of the Arab crews using them. By the mid-1970s, the Soviet Army had already begun replacing its T62s with newer generations of tanks.

With the signing of a number of arms control treaties, both the former USSR and its Warsaw Pact Allies agreed to scrap most of their older generation tanks, including the T62. As a result, there are currently six T62 tanks now in private hands. For the collector, they share many of the same good and bad points with the T54/55 tanks. Because they are both a newer and more advanced vehicle than the T54/55 tank, a fully restored T62 might go for $30,000, whereas an operational vehicle might sell for only $20,000.

M60 Medium Tank

The most modern Army tank available to collectors is the M60 medium tank. This tank is not for sale, but the Army museum system has been authorized to trade M60s to any private collector who may have a rare vehicle

that Army museums can't afford to buy and need to fill out their historical collections.

The first M60 tank was basically an improved late-model M48 medium tank. The Army was fairly happy with the 90mm-gun-armed M48 series of tanks, but this changed when the USSR in late 1947 introduced the T54 tank armed with a 100mm gun. On paper, the T54 seemed to be superior to the M48, prompting the Army to hurriedly build an improved M48 tank with a bigger gun. Fortunately, the British had already developed a new 105mm gun, which, after the breech was redesigned, was mounted onto a heavily modified M48A2 tank with a new front hull and a diesel engine. The M48A2 was then redesignated the M60 tank.

Although the new M60 was obviously just an improved M48, it was never called a "Patton tank." It looked very much like the M48 tank, but there were several distinguishing features, including a flat front hull plate, a larger cupola for the tank commander, a 105mm gun with a bore evacuator half-way

The Israeli Army made extensive use of the M60A1 tanks during the 1973 Yom Kippur War. This vehicle has been hit and destroyed by Egyptian anti-tank weapons. *Egyptian Army*

down the barrel, and redesigned road wheels and fenders.

The first-production M60 tanks were sent to Army units in Western Europe in late 1960. While the Army was very happy with its new 105mm gun-equipped tank, it was not satisfied with the turret shape and began work on a turret with a better ballistic shape that could deflect newer Soviet antitank weapons. In 1962, a newer turret was fitted to an M60 hull. This new turret featured an elongated nose, which provided better ballistic protection, as well as a pronounced rear bustle, making much more interior space available to the four-man crew. The Army designated this new variant of the M60 tank the M60A1 tank to reflect the major changes.

The M60 weighed about 58 tons, and was 22ft 9in long, 11ft 11in wide, and 10ft 8in tall. Powered by various improved versions of a Continental twelve-cylinder, air-cooled diesel engine, the M60 had a top speed of about 30mph and an operational range of approximately 310 miles.

As time went on, the M60A1 was continuously improved to keep it up to par with enemy tank developments. In addition to the Army and the USMC, several friendly governments were either given or sold M60A1 tanks. The biggest user of M60A1 tanks in combat was the Israeli Army. During the 1973 Yom Kippur War, the American-built M60A1 was the backbone of the Israeli armed forces. The M60A1 performed very well against

In service with the Army for only a few years, the M103 heavy tank was first fielded in 1956, but by the early 1960s, it was replaced by the M60 medium tank with a 105mm cannon. The M103 weighed about 60 tons and mounted a very long-barreled 120mm cannon. The vehicle pictured is being tested in the water tank at Aberdeen Proving Grounds, Maryland, in May 1954. *US Army*

Pictured is the driver's compartment of the M103 heavy tank. *Michael Green*

modern Soviet-supplied Arab tanks, but the very lower front of the its turret was too thin. Extra armor was added to later-production models to strengthen the turret in that area.

By 1978, another large upgrading of the M60A1 led to its reclassification as the M60A3. Still in use, the M60A3 has several unique features, especially the M1-tank-type fire-control system, which includes a laser range finder, solid state electronic computer, and tank thermal sight.

Since the beginning of its production run in early 1960, the M60 series was considered to be only an interim vehicle intended to serve the Army until the ideal tank could be designed and built. But, 15,000 tanks later, it is still being used by the Army National Guard and by the USMC. The USMC used M60s during Operation Desert Storm. It's hoped by 1997 that M1 or M1A1 tanks will replace all

While the Army stopped using M103s after only a short time, the USMC continued to use them until the early 1970s. The very long overhang of the 120mm cannon can be seen on this M103, belonging to a private collector. *Michael Green*

Produced too late to see action during WWII, the British-built Centurion tank first saw action during the Korean War. Pictured is a 52-ton Centurion tank of the British forces, crossing an American-built pontoon bridge in Korea on June 7, 1951. *US Army*

remaining M60A3 tanks in the American inventory.

In foreign service, the M60 series has seen its most extensive combat with the Israeli Army. M60s were also used by Iran during its exhaustive eight-year war with Iraq, and are currently used in large numbers by the armies of Saudi Arabia, Egypt, Thailand, Jordan, Austria, Italy, and Taiwan.

For collectors who want to trade a historic vehicle to the Army for an M60 series tank, be aware that the size and weight of the vehicle is a serious drawback. The powerpack alone,

weighs in at 5 tons. While the powerpack can be removed from the vehicle's hull and placed on blocks for ease of maintenance. This can be done only with heavy-duty cranes and the help of at least two people.

Because of the complex nature of the M60's turret components and fire-control systems. The Army had specially trained mechanics just to maintain them. A typical collector might have a hard time keeping the turret on an M60 working without the right training.

Parts for the M60 series are a little expensive at the moment. However, as the Army

79

The Centurion was a huge sales success for the British arms industry. Dozens of other armies adopted various versions of the vehicle. Pictured on parade are two Centurions of the Indian Army. *Chris Foss photo*

continues to scrap their fleet of M60s, the price of parts may come down.

US M103 Heavy Tank

During the opening stages of the Korean War (1950 to 1953), 150 Soviet-supplied T34/85 tanks of the North Korean Army in conjunction with 100,000 North Korean infantrymen almost completely overran South Korea. Both South Korea and American military units were brushed aside by the Soviet-built tanks.

Fearing that the Korean War would escalate into a worldwide conflict, the Army quickly realized that most of its tank fleet was obsolete. To deal with newer generations of Soviet heavy tanks, such as the IS-3 and T10M armed with 122mm cannons, the Army rushed into production a prototype heavy tank known as the T43. Armed with a 120mm cannon, this vehicle later became known as

the M103. The Army ordered 300 for itself and the USMC from the manufacturer, Chrysler Corporation. Production was completed by 1954, but early testing problems delayed the tank's introduction into field units until 1956.

When finally deployed into service, the M103 was the largest tank ever used by the American military. It was 22ft 11in long, 12ft 4in wide, and 9ft 5in tall, and weighed almost 60 tons.

In the mid-1950s, the military envisioned that the M103 would use its long-range 120mm gun to engage Soviet heavy tanks, while the M47 and M48 medium tanks armed with only 90mm guns would do battle with Soviet medium tanks. It didn't work that way. By the early 1960s, the M103 was replaced in Army service by the newer M60 series of main battle tanks, armed with very powerful 105mm guns that equaled the performance of the larger 120mm guns. For all practical purposes, the distinction between medium and heavy tanks disappeared; the Soviet Army also later stopped building heavy tanks as the guns on its former medium tanks also became more capable.

The USMC, which has always had less money to spend on equipment than the Army, continued to use the M103 until the early 1970s, when additional supplies of M60 tanks allowed it to put its M103s into storage.

In its original form, the M103 was basically an M48 with a lengthened hull, the same engine, and a 120mm gun mounted in a very large, elongated cast-steel armor turret. This large turret carried four crewmen; the driver sat in the front center of the hull. Unlike most American tanks, the M103 commander and the gunner both sat in the very long, rear-overhanging bustle of the turret. Because of their size, rounds for the 120mm gun were loaded in two parts, a process requiring two loaders instead of the normal single loader found in all other US tanks. On both sides of the main gun were .30cal coaxially mounted machine guns. The vehicle commander's hatch was also fitted with a .50cal machine gun. The M103 could carry thirty-three separated rounds of 120mm ammunition.

The M103 was powered by a twelve-cylin-

The Israeli Army was the best-known user of the Centurion tank in combat. Pictured on the Golan Heights during the 1973 Yom Kippur War is an Israeli Army Centurion mounting a 105mm cannon. *Israeli Army*

A replacement for the Centurion, the British Army's Chieftain main battle tank was first fielded in 1967. Armed with a large 120mm rifled tank cannon and protected by well-shaped and very thick armor, the Chieftain has only recently been retired from British Army service. The tank shown was based in West Berlin and had an urban-style camouflage scheme. *Michael Green*

der Continental air-cooled gas engine producing 810hp at 2,800rpm. With a fuel capacity of 280gal, the M103 used 3gal of gas for every mile it traveled, resulting in an 80-mile operational range. Top was 21mph.

In USMC service, the M103 was upgraded with an improved fire-control system and the same diesel engine as fitted in the M60 tank. With the Continental AVDS-17902A diesel engine, the operational range of the M103 went from 80 miles to almost 300 miles. In this final configuration, the M103 became the M103A3.

Only two M103s have made it into collectors' hands. Never exported to any foreign country, most M103s eventually became targets on military target ranges.

Unless you have a very large garage, the M103 is not the tank for you. The M103 is a vehicle you would buy for its rarity and to place it on display, not to drive around in the hills behind your home. And unless, you have another vehicle as large and as powerful to act as a recovery vehicle, a breakdown in your M103 means it is going to stay there a long time.

Prices on M103s start at $20,000 for a hulk, $50,000 to $60,000 for an operational model, and $80,000 or more for a fully restored vehicle.

British Centurion Tank

One of the best-known British tanks of the postwar era is the Centurion. First developed during the closing stages of WWII, the Centurion has been upgraded and improved countless times to keep pace with other countries' tanks. Still seeing limited service with the British military, the Centurion has been in more than twenty different models, not counting the variants.

The Centurion first saw combat during the Korean War. However, it is best known for its combat use with the Israeli Army. During Israel's numerous wars with its Arab neighbors, the Centurion defeated the Soviet and American tank used by its opponents.

Originally designed as a tank able to defeat later-war German tanks such as the Panther and Tigers, the Centurion's basic design has resoundingly withstood the test of time. Only within the last decade have newer tank designs pushed the Centurion into storage or surplus yards.

The hull of the Centurion is made of weld-

Because the PT-76 was designed to be fully amphibious, it had a very large boat-like shape. To
keep it lightweight, its armor protection was very

thin; heavy machine gun fire could easily penetrate
it. *Greg Stewart*

ed-steel armor. The front hull is well-sloped
and about 5in thick. The turret consists of
cast-steel armor with a welded-steel armor
roof. There is an ammunition re-supply hatch
in the left side of the turret.

All models of the Centurion have a four-
man crew. The vehicle commander has a
counter-rotating cupola that allows him to
turn it 360deg independent of the turret direction. The cupola has a single-piece hatch
cover, a periscope sight, and seven periscopes
which afford him the utmost in visibility
without having to expose his upper body out
of the turret.

Throughout its service in the British Army,
the Centurion was powered by a Rolls-Royce
Meteor twelve-cylinder, liquid-cooled gas engine. The Centurion had a top speed of about
21mph and an operational range of 125 miles.
It wasn't until the Israeli Army modified its
fleet of Centurions with American-made
750hp Continental diesel engines that the
Centurion's speed and operational range
equaled that of other countries' tanks. Top

speed was now about 32mph and operational
range was almost 200 miles.

The most important aspect of the Centurion tank design throughout its service life has
been the British desire to mount the most
powerful tank gun possible. The first Centurions were fitted with 17-pounder tank guns.
British troops sent to Korea in 1950 had Centurion tanks armed with 20-pounder guns.

In 1957, the Centurion tank was armed
with a 105mm British-designed tank-gun. The
105mm offered a 25 percent better chance of
hitting a target than the earlier 20lb, combined
with improvements in its fire-control system.
The Centurion tank with the 105mm gun was
equal if not better than most Soviet tanks of
the 1960s and 1970s. Later models of the Centurion were fitted with state-of-the-art night-
vision equipment, including both infrared
and, later, passive night sights.

The Australian Army used a fleet of Centurion tanks for many years. In early 1968,
about a dozen were sent to South Vietnam to
support Australian units already stationed

there. After proving their worth in battles with the Vietcong, the Australian military deployed additional Centurions to fight in Vietnam. The Centurions never saw action against NVA tanks, but their heavy armor and firepower proved invaluable in supporting infantry operations.

Austria no longer uses the Centurion tank with its armored units. The Austrian Army removed the turrets of many of the Centurions and dug them in as static pillboxes to defend the country in case of attack.

South Africa has a fleet of more than 300 Centurion tanks, a few of which saw action in Angola. Because modern tanks are so expensive, South Africa followed Israel's example and recently upgraded its Centurions with diesel engines, additional armor protection, solid-state fire-control equipment, and other improvements.

The British built 4,423 Centurions of various models between 1945 and 1962, of which about half were exported. As more armies have replaced their Centurions during the last couple of decades, many have become range targets. Some, like those of the Australian Army, were sold to an Australian equipment dealer who bought the entire fleet. A few of these vehicles, as well as former-Canadian Centurions that were sold as surplus, have now appeared in collectors' hands.

This photo of a PT-76 shows the two water jets mounted at the rear of the hull. The vehicle was steered in the water by opening and closing the two armored doors located over the water jet opening. On this PT-76, the doors are closed. *Michael Green*

As of 1993, the British military decided that its entire stock of war-reserve Centurion tanks was surplus to its needs. As a result, fully operational Centurion tanks from the final upgrade period are now available for the unheard price of $10,000 each. This makes the Centurion the cheapest tank on the collector's market at the moment. Parts are also available at very reasonable prices. Prior to this sell-off, the price for an operational vehicle was at least $40,000. A fully restored model would sell for $70,000. Some of the vehicles coming out of the British Army storage sheds are a little rough, but the price cannot be beat. The biggest problem for interested collectors in the United States will be paying for the shipping costs of this 50-ton vehicle. Another problem with buying a Centurion tank is that you need a large storage area and heavy-duty maintenance equipment. Having lots of friends who are willing to get their hands dirty would also be a big help.

British Chieftain Tank

Even though the Centurion was an excellent tank, new developments in firepower, armor protection, and mobility eventually render all tanks obsolete. The British Army was well aware that the postwar Soviet Army had a massive fleet of very effective tanks and was constantly improving them or building newer models. To keep pace with Soviet tank developments, the British decided to build a tank with the most powerful gun possible, supported by the thickest armor protection that could be mounted on a tracked vehicle while retaining a certain level of battlefield mobility.

By the early 1960s, they built a number of prototype vehicles that came to be known as the Chieftain. The Chieftain was of conventional tank design, with a driver in the front hull and a commander, gunner, and loader in a turret in the middle of the hull. The engine gearbox and transmission were in the rear of the hull.

To give their tank an edge over enemy vehicles, the British mounted a very accurate, high-velocity 120mm gun in the turret. Because of the size and weight of the 120mm rounds (almost 40lb), they used a bagged-charge system. This meant that the 120mm

Developed shortly after WWII by Soviet tank designers was the PT-76 light amphibious tank. Almost 7,000 were built between the early 1950s and the late 1960s. The vehicle has seen widespread combat action in the Middle East, Africa, Asia, and India. *Michael Green*

ammunition came in two pieces: the actual projectile that shot out of the barrel and the powder that exploded in the firing chamber and pushed the warhead out the barrel. While this system did slow down the Chieftain's rate of fire, the superior accuracy and lethality of the 120mm gun in the Chieftain more than made up for its slightly slower rate of fire. The 120mm gun itself was almost 19ft long and weighed close to 2 tons. As with most postwar British tanks, the Chieftain's 120mm gun was fully stabilized in both elevation and traverse.

Combat loaded, the Chieftain tank weighed about 54 tons. Like the Centurion tanks, the Chieftain rode on a Hosetman-type suspension system and came in a number of different models, each an improvement over its immediate predecessor. The standard Chieftain engine was known as the Leyland L60 six-cylinder multi-fuel, which produced about 750hp, giving the vehicle a top speed of about 30mph and an operational range of more than 250 miles. Unfortunately, the Leyland L60 engine never lived up to its expectations, its engine causing constant problems.

While many modifications were made over the years, the engine continued to suffer too-frequent failures.

The Chieftain tank was 24ft 8in long, 11ft 6in wide, and 9ft 6in tall. Armor protection was outstanding. When the Chieftain finally reached the British Army tank units in 1967, it had probably the thickest armor of any tank then in operational service. To improve its armor protection, both the turret and hull of the vehicle were highly sloped. The Chieftain's well-sloped hull armor also added to its level of immunity from antitank mines. To increase the front hull slope, the driver's seat was placed in a prone position with hatches down, allowing a lower silhouette for the vehicle. Like the Centurion, the Chieftain was also fitted with thin armor plates on either side of the hull to either side of the vehicle's

hull to help deflect infantry antitank weapons.

As with most modern tanks of both the Western and Soviet armies, the Chieftain was fitted with a Nuclear, Biological, and Chemical (NBC) ventilation system as protection against nuclear fallout or bacteriological or chemical attacks.

By the time production ended in the early 1970s, 900 Chieftains had been built. With the end of the Cold War and the reduction of armored forces throughout Europe, most of the British Army Chieftains are scheduled to be scrapped and used as range targets.

As they have with the Centurion, the British military has slowly started to release a number of Chieftain tanks from its war-reserve stocks. Their price is also about $10,000. However, the 60-ton Chieftain has all the

Shown in Israeli Army service, this early-model AMX 13 light tank, armed with a 75mm cannon, is taking part in a 1960 training exercise. In the 1967 Six Day War, Israeli AMX 13 tanks suffered heavy losses, due to their light armor protection. Shortly afterwards, Israel sold its entire fleet of AMX 13 tanks to Singapore. *Israeli Army*

same pitfalls in ownership as the Centurion does and a few more to boot. Being a more modern vehicle than the Centurion, it has a large number of very complex turret systems that an untrained collector would have great difficulty in maintaining. Spare parts including engines are very hard to find for the vehicle. Despite these drawbacks the vehicle is a very impressive display piece.

Soviet PT-76 Amphibious Tank

Entering Soviet military service in the early 1950s, the PT-76 was a lightly armored amphibious tank with a flat, boat-like hull housing a dish-type turret on which a 76.2mm main gun was mounted. A coaxial 7.62mm machine gun was mounted at the right of the main gun.

The PT-76 was formerly the standard reconnaissance tank of the Warsaw Pact armies. The PT-76 still serves in a number of foreign armies.

The American military first encountered the PT-76 during the Vietnam War. In a surprise attack in 1967, several NVA PT-76s tried to overrun the Army Special Forces Camp at Lang Vei. Beaten back, the NVA attacked the same camp the next year, this time successfully. Seven of the ten PT-76 tanks that overran the camp were destroyed with antitank rockets. In March 1969, eight PT-76s attacked the Special Forces Camp at Ben Het. This time, they ran into a defending platoon of five American M48 Patton tanks armed with 90mm guns. In the ensuing battle, the PT-76 tanks managed to damage only a single Patton tank and lost two of their own, before beating a hasty retreat. This was the only time that American tanks did battle with NVA tanks during the entire Vietnamese War.

During the very early stages of the 1973 Yom Kippur War between Israel and its Arab neighbors, Egyptian PT-76 tanks swam across the Suez Canal in an attempt to seize Israeli Army positions. The very thin armor of the PT-76s gave them very little protection from Israeli main gun fire and most were quickly destroyed.

The PT-76 was rather large and thinly armored for its weight, but this was necessary since the tank was designed to be completely amphibious. In the water, the PT-76 was pro-

In the early 1960s, the French began to up-gun their AMX 13 light tanks with a 90mm cannon. The 90mm cannon barrel was fitted with a thermal sleeve to improve firing accuracy. The vehicle pictured was donated by the French Army to the Patton Museum at Fort Knox, Kentucky. *Michael Green*

pelled by two water jets at the rear of the hull.

The hull and turret of the PT-76 tank were less than 1in thick, making it vulnerable to artillery fragments and .50cal machine gun fire. The driver sat at the front of the hull, and the engine and transmission are in the rear hull. The engine was a water-cooled, in-line, six-cylinder diesel that could reach 240hp at 1800rpm. This enabled the tank to reach speeds of 35mph on level ground and have an operational range of about 210 miles.

During its time in service, the PT-76 was fitted with a variety of different 76mm main guns, the gun itself a development of the 76mm gun found on early model T34 medium tanks used during WWII. Early models mounted a gun with no bore evacuator and a long multislotted muzzle brake. Later models mounted a 76mm gun with a bore evacuator and a double-baffle muzzle brake. Newer versions of the PT-76 had a lighter, stabilized 76mm gun.

Overall, the PT-76 was a reliable, highly mobile reconnaissance vehicle. China manufactures a very similar amphibious tank known as the T-60.

Most PT-76 tanks available on the collectors' market have been former-Egyptian military vehicles. When Egypt began re-equipping with only Western AFVs, its PT-76 tanks were declared surplus and sold for scrap.

The PT-76 is a nice vehicle to own since it is both light and historical. On the negative side, parts may be hard to find. There are less than five PT-76s in private hands. Prices for an operational vehicle start at $15,000, while a fully restored vehicle would go for $25,000.

French AMX 13 Tank

At the end of WWII, the Free French Army was primarily equipped with American-made AFVs such as the M4 Sherman. In an effort to develop its own tank-building industry again, the French Army drafted requirements for a number of new tanks. One vehicle was to be a light tank with a powerful gun, which could be flown by transport plane to any of France's overseas possessions. Unfortunately, the French Air Force never deployed an aircraft that could carry such a vehicle. Nevertheless, the new light tank built for the French Army, turned out to be a very successful design. The new tank made its debut in 1951 and was known as the AMX 13. This tank served in at least twenty-six other countries' armies, and still serves some today. Total production for the AMX 13 was about 5,000 vehicles.

The original AMX 13 weighed about 15 tons, and was armed with a shortened version of the 75mm gun found on the Panther tank. Later versions of the AMX 13 featured a 90mm gun. Because it has been designed as a light tank, the armor protection on the AMX 13 was fairly thin; the turret would stop 20mm rounds, but most of the tank was protected only against small arms fire up to .50cal.

The AMX 13 was powered by an eight-cylinder, water-cooled gas engine that gave it a top speed of 40mph. Operational range was about 220 miles. In addition to its main gun, the AMX 13 had a coaxial machine gun mounted in the turret.

The AMX 13 had a three-man crew. Its most unusual feature was its oscillating turret. Unlike the typical tank with a one-piece turret, in which the main gun has to be raised or lowered by machinery, the AMX 13 had a two-piece turret. The top part, containing the main gun and crew, was mounted in trunnions in the bottom, fixed part, so that the upper turret was raised or lowered by moving the entire unit. The bottom part of the AMX 13 turret rotated in azimuth.

American tank designers had also briefly tried out the oscillating turret concept but rejected it because of numerous technical problems. However, while not a perfect design, the AMX 13 did have a very good reputation for reliability—although working on the engine could be a problem since it was cramped very tightly into the front hull.

Because the AMX 13 turret-mounted main gun did not have to move within the turret, the main gun could be mounted very close to the turret roof. This made the AMX 13 a shorter target, at 7ft 7in tall.

For collectors who want a smaller, lightweight tank, the AMX 13 is an attractive option in a postwar tank design. There are plenty of spare parts around. However, since the AMX 13 still serves in many armies, the parts are very expensive to buy. An AMX hulk starts at $5,000 and goes up to $15,000 for an operational vehicle. A fully restored vehicle could go for $25,000. There are only two AMX 13 tanks currently in private hands.

Chapter 4

Armored Personnel Carriers

German Sdkfz 251/OT-810

During the final years of World War I, the German Army had under development its first troop-carrying half-track. The vehicle never went into production, and it wasn't until the mid-1920s that the Germans began testing a number of trucks and half-tracks. They decided that half-tracks offered superior cross-country mobility over wheeled vehicles and in the early 1930s bought several unarmored half-tracks to tow artillery guns. By the mid-1930s, the German Army was beginning to lay down the foundations of its new *panzer* divisions. It needed an AFV that could carry a ten-man squad of soldiers. The solution was an armored version of a 3-ton artillery-towing vehicle.

Fitted with a very well-angled armored hull, this new troop-carrying half-track was known as the Sdkfz 251. Production began in 1939 and the Sdkfz 251 saw its first action during the invasion of Poland in September

Shortly before WWII started, the German Army fielded a half-track-based APC known as the Sdkfz 251 series. Built on the chassis of an unarmored artillery-towing vehicle, it proved to be a very successful vehicle and was modified for a variety of different roles. Pictured in North Africa is this early-model Sdkfz 251 used as a command and control vehicle mounting a large-frame aerial. *German Army*

On display at a museum in Germany is this late-model Sdkfz 251 series half-track configured as an APC. In addition to the weapons of its onboard troops, these vehicles normally mounted two machine guns for protection. *Richard A. Pemberton*

1939. So successful were these new APCs that the German Army mandated that all of its motorized infantry units be equipped with these vehicles as soon as possible.

German factories built almost 15,000 various models of the Sdkfz 251 and its twenty-two different official variants, but there were never enough to equip all the German units that needed them.

The Sdkfz 251s carried a two-man crew—the driver and vehicle commander—plus a ten-man infantry squad. It weighed a little under 8 tons, and was 19ft long, 6ft 10-1/2in wide, and 5ft 9in tall. Powered by a six-cylinder, water-cooled gas engine, the Sdkfz 251 could reach a top speed of 33mph and had an operational range of about 180 miles.

Its armor protection was proof only against small arms fire. The rear personnel compartment was open-topped, allowing the occupants to escape over the sides or through two large rear doors. The Sdkfz 251 was normally fitted with at least two machine guns located in the front and rear; the troops could also fire their own weapons over the sides.

Like most AFVs, the Sdkfz 251 was constantly improved as the war went on. There were four basic production models, each a simplification of its earlier version. Overall, they were all very similar except for external detail differences. Normally, the vehicles were made out of welded-steel, but there were a number built of riveted construction.

During WWII, a number of Czechoslovakian factories, under German control, were used to produce the Sdkfz 251. After the war ended, the Czech Army took into service a large supply of former-German equipment, including several Sdkfz 251s. In the mid-1950s, the Czechs decided to develop and build their own improved version of the Sdkfz 251 APC. The new vehicle would be known as the OT-810.

Production of the OT-810 began in 1959 and ended in 1963, with a total of 1,500 vehicles being built. The Czech vehicle looked very much like its original predecessor except it had an air-cooled, eight-cylinder diesel engine and overhead protection for the crew compartment. Also added were thicker armor and firing ports in the hull sides. Like the German version, the OT-810 came in many different variations, including a command and control vehicle and an antitank vehicle on which an 82mm recoilless rifle was mounted.

By the 1970s, the OT-810 series was beginning to show its age. Compared to newer, fully tracked APCs, the OT-810 was obsolete, and beginning in the early 1980s, most were either scrapped or placed into storage. A few passed into private hands, where they were heavily modified for farm use. At least one OT-810 was sold to a British vehicle dealer in 1988. With the collapse of the USSR and its various Warsaw Pact Allies, several countries now have a huge amount of unneeded AFVs. As a result, many OT-810s are now for sale. At least one has made it into the United States, where it has now been converted to look like the original German version, and at least two dozen are in private collectors' hands in Europe and Great Britain. There is at least one restored Sdkfz 251 in private hands, with maybe another five vehicles ranging from hulk to operational condition also in private hands.

There is a big difference in prices between the German wartime models of the Sdkfz 251 and the post-war Czech-built OT-810. A Sdkfz 251 hulk may go for $30,000, while an operational vehicle would go for up to $50,000. A fully restored Sdkfz 251 could sell from $70,000 and up because of its rarity. In contrast, an operational OT-810 can be had for $15,000, with a fully restored example going for about $25,000.

According to collectors who already own OT-810s, the vehicle is a lot of fun to drive. The diesel engine runs very well. Unfortunately, the exhaust vents for the engine are located on the front of the vehicle, which means that you get a constant stream of choking diesel exhaust in your face. Parts are almost impossible to get, making them difficult to repair.

M2 and M3 Half-Tracks

The most common AFV found in collectors' hands is the American-built M2 and M3 half-tracks, which were used throughout WWII by the Allied armies and are still used in far-flung corners of the world.

Two basic families of American half-tracks were built during WWII. One family (M2, M2A1, M3, and M3A1)was designed and built by the White Motor Co., which licensed two other American truck companies, Diamond T Motor Car Co. and the Autocar Co., to build identical copies. Almost 40,000 half-tracks were built by these three companies between 1941 and 1944. The other family of half-tracks (M5, M5A1, M9, and M9A1) was built by the famous tractor builder, International Harvester. International Harvester built almost 14,000 improved copies of the White Motor Co. design for the Allies, especially England and the USSR.

The Army had experimented with unarmored half-tracks as early as World War I, but the idea of an armored half-track didn't appear until 1937. It was the Cavalry Depart-

The Sdkfz 251 series of half-tracks were thinly armored. This one has been hit by Allied ground-attack aircraft and is burning. *National Archives*

ment that expressed initial interest in a half-track vehicle to carry personnel. Realizing that horses were of little use in modern warfare, the cavalry had already begun to use wheeled armored scout cars during the 1930s. Their use had convinced the cavalry that a half-track, with its improved off-road mobility, could be used to scout and tow artillery guns. In 1938, the Army's Ordnance Branch modified the chassis of a White Motor Co.-built M2A1 wheeled scout car to accommodate a half-track assembly. Known as the T7, this vehicle wasn't perfect. It lacked powered front wheels and didn't have enough storage space. White Motor tried again the next year, producing a prototype vehicle known as the White Motor Co. T14 Half-Track Armored Car. WWII had already started in September 1939 with the German invasion of Poland. The widespread use of half-tracks by the German Army as APCs and in other roles such as command and control vehicles greatly impressed the American military leaders. The Army immediately accepted the T14 into service in September 1940 as the Half-Track Armored Car M2. Two additional variants were

The use of captured equipment by soldiers of all armies is very common. This WWII-era picture shows American soldiers using two captured German Army Sdkfz 251 series half-tracks. The soldiers have placed a variety of markings on the vehicles so that they won't be shot by their own troops. *National Archives*

After WWII, the Czech Army began building its own version of the German Sdkfz 251 series half-track, known as the OT-810, which has started to appear in the hands of private collectors. This vehicle is owned by Grant Kruger and has been painted and marked to resemble a German Army half-track from WWII. *Richard A. Pemberton*

Following the German lead, the Army quickly began deploying a large number of armored half-tracks early in WWII. Like the German armored half-tracks, the new American armored half-tracks were based on the unarmored artillery-towing vehicle. Pictured is the ancestor of the American WWII armored half-tracks, the T5 artillery mover, on a training exercise in 1935. *US Army*

The thin armor and lack of overhead protection on the American half-tracks of WWII made them very unpopular with the troops using them. American soldiers nicknamed them "Purple Heart Boxes" in grim reference to the Army decoration for being wounded in combat. The M3 half-track pictured is taking part in a large training exercise in the United States in late 1942. *US Army*

planned, one being the Half-Track Personnel Carrier M3, which had a longer hull and greater seating capacity than the M2, and the Half-Track Mortar Carrier M4, which mounted an 81mm mortar in the rear hull compartment.

American-built half-tracks were essentially nothing more than modified civilian truck chassis, with short track-laying units in place of rear wheels. Adding a thin steel armor hull, the Army had a vehicle it could build cheaply and in large numbers. While the half-tracks' off-road mobility didn't compare to that of fully tracked vehicles, they were a big improvement over wheeled trucks. They were also a lot easier to maintain and operate in the field than fully tracked vehicles.

The Army quickly realized the versatility of the half-track and began to see it as an all-purpose combat vehicle that could carry a wide variety of weapon systems and perform a number of different duties.

The most common use of the half-track by the Army during WWII was as an APC. In this role, the M3 half-track had seating for a driver and twelve infantrymen. A rear door provided easy access or escape. The M3 car-

ried on a pedestal mount a .50cal machine gun, and there were pintle socket mounts for additional machine guns. The troops could also use their own small arms through the open top if necessary. The M3 was also used to carry ammo for artillery units and as an armored ambulance for the wounded.

The M2 had no rear access door and its machine gun armament was mounted on a skate ring around the entire upper inside hull. Smaller than the M3, the M2 could not carry a full infantry squad, but it could act as a command vehicle, tow artillery or antitank guns, or mount a mortar in its rear hull.

Armor protection on all half-tracks was no thicker than 1/4in overall and 1/2in on the windshield. The half-track's thin armor and open-topped design made it very unpopular with most infantrymen, who nicknamed it the "Purple Heart Box."

American half-tracks used a vertical volute-spring suspension system riding on an endless band track 12in wide with a 4in pitch. The track was supported by one support roller accompanied by four bogie wheels per side. This gave the vehicle fairly good flexibility for off-road conditions. It also had a front-wheeled semi-elliptic spring axle, enabling only the front wheels to be steered by a cam and lever system.

The typical M3 half-track was powered by a six-cylinder, in-line, water-cooled White Motor Co. 160AX gas engine of 147hp. Top speed was about 45mph. Operational range was approximately 216 miles. The M3 could climb 32deg slopes and cross 12in vertical obstacles. It was 20ft 3.5in long (about 10in longer than the M2), 6ft 9in tall, and 7ft 1in wide. Combat loaded, the M3 weighed about 7 tons.

M3 half-tracks were normally assigned to Army mechanized infantry platoons, one half-track per rifle squad. During WWII, there could be as many as 800 half-tracks in an Army tank division. Half-tracks would typically carry infantry in close support of tanks until opposing artillery or antitank fire became too heavy. At this point, the infantry were supposed to dismount and attack on foot, but the infantry would sometimes follow the tanks right into battle and fight from their vehicles.

The British Army received almost 6,000 American half-tracks during WWII. They tended to use them as armored utility vehicles or to tow their antitank guns.

Like tanks, the American-built half-tracks were modified in various details during production. Each modification resulted in a new designation by the Army. An example is the M3, which later became the M3A1, M3A2, M3A3, and M3A4. The International Harvester-built version of the M3 half-track personnel carrier was known as the M5. It was powered by an International Red 450B six-cylinder, in-line, gas engine. Like the M3, the M5 was later modified and was redesignated the M5A1. International Harvester also built its own version of the M2 and M2A1 half-track armored car known as the M9A1. These International Harvester-built half-tracks could be easily distinguished from the M3 variations by the rounded rear corners of their hulls and their flat fenders.

The Army used many variations of the basic M3 half-track during WWII, including a tank destroyer with a 75mm gun mounted in its center. Known as the 75mm Gun Motor Carriage M3 and M3A1, this vehicle was first used in North Africa by the Army. It was outclassed by German tanks, and saw its most effective use with American soldiers fighting the Japanese Army where the threat from Japanese tanks was almost nil.

The most common half-track armament consisted of a variety of antiaircraft gun systems. Ranging from two to four .50cal machine guns up to 40mm antiaircraft guns, the first of these was the M13 half-track, which mounted in its rear hull compartment a

Because of early combat experience, several modifications were made to the M2 and M3 half-tracks. The most visible feature was the adoption of the M49 machine gun mount. This pulpit-type mount was fitted to the right front of the vehicle beside the driver, allowing easier use of machine guns against low-flying aircraft. In this configuration, the half-tracks now became the M2A1 and M3A1. Pictured is an M3A1 half-track belonging to a private collector. *Michael Green*

Because so many American-built half-tracks of WWII survived into civilian work, many have come into private collectors' hands. Being of a very simple design, they are relatively easy to restore to operational condition. Pictured is an M16 half-track being restored by a private collector.

power-operated, one-man turret armed with twin .50cal machine guns. Combat experience showed that additional firepower was needed, so a new vehicle, known as the M15 and M15A1, was built. This half-track was armed with twin .50cal machine guns and a 37mm cannon. Later developments included a power-operated, one-man turret incorporating four instead of two .50cal machine guns. Designed to protect American soldiers and their vehicles from low-flying attack aircraft, this vehicle was standardized as the M16 in Army service.

Other versions of the M3 half-track family included the M21 81mm mortar carrier, the T30 75mm howitzer motor carriage, and the T48 half-track armed with a 57mm antitank gun.

American half-track production ended in 1944. At the end of the war, most of the Army's inventory of half-tracks was declared surplus and supplied to the Allies or sold as surplus in the United States. Because of its simple construction, the half-track, stripped of its armor and guns, found a number of civilian occupations from dump trucks to salt spreaders. Those half-tracks remaining in the Army inventory after WWII were mostly converted into carrying the M45 (quad .50cal machine gun) mount and were then designated M16A1 for the Korean War. After the Korean War, a few half-tracks could be found in National Guard units until the late 1950s.

The biggest postwar combat user of the American-built half-tracks was the Israeli Army, which used modified half-tracks until the late 1980s. The Israeli Army found the half-track a most useful chassis and mounted a vast number of different types of armaments on it. In addition to weapons carriers, Israeli half-tracks were used as command and control vehicles with raised roofs, ambu-

The last half-track passed out of Army service shortly after the Korean War, but was retained for use by numerous armies around the world until very recently. The largest user of postwar half-tracks has been Israel. Of the many modifications done to the half-tracks by the Israelis, the most noticeable was a machine gun position added to the right of the driver's seat—which can be seen in this picture of an Israeli Army half-track during a peace-time training exercise. *Israeli Army*

lances, and ammunition and cargo carriers. Sometime during the late 1970s, the Israelis replaced the earlier gas engine with the Detroit Diesel 6V52 diesel engine (the same as used in the M113) coupled to an Allison TX-100N automatic transmission and a Spicer gearbox.

Currently, half-tracks of various types can be found in both unrestored and restorable shape. Israel is also releasing some of its rebuilt (diesel-engine) half-tracks to the collectors' market. Because of its long time in foreign military service and the large number of vehicles released into civilian hands, parts for half-tracks tend to be readily available from a number of sources.

There are at least 350 to 500 various types of half-tracks now in private hands. Hulk prices start at $3,000 and go up to $15,000 for an operational vehicle. A fully restored vehicle may sell for $20,000 to $25,000.

The biggest problem with the half-track is its original rear tracks. They have a very short lifespan because of their WWII design and now their age. They are in short supply and tend to be very expensive when they can be

found. Because the half-tracks are such popular vehicles among collectors and can be driven on the highway. Their rear tracks are subject to a level of use that they weren't designed for. A number of serious incidents have occurred when the rear tracks on a half-track snapped and fell apart at high speed (30mph). There are now a few collectors who have started to make new tracks to keep their vehicles running.

British Bren Carrier

In contrast to US and German development of half-tracks before and during WWII, the British had begun experiments in the mid-1930s on a number of small, fully tracked, open-topped vehicles designed primarily as APCs but also able to mount infantry weapons or to tow wheeled guns.

By 1938, the British had decided to begin production of a vehicle known as the Bren Carrier, originally configured to carry a light machine gun and three-man crew. It was used in the mechanized cavalry regiments of the British Army. Other versions soon followed, including a personnel carrier that could accommodate six men and an armored carrier for the forward observation officers of the British artillery units.

The carrier was only 4ft 9in tall, 12ft long, and 6ft 9in wide. Made by a number of British factories, the carrier was powered by a Ford V-8 gas engine which gave it a top speed of 30mph and an operational range of fewer than 100 miles.

Despite their many shortcomings, the American-built half-tracks of WWII were easy and cheap to build in large numbers. Pictured in an English field, prior to D-day, is a storage site filled with hundreds of half-tracks. *National Archives*

After WWII, the Universal Carrier (still called the Bren by most soldiers) was used by many armies, including the Israeli Army. Pictured are two Israeli Army Universal Carriers in 1948. *Israeli Army*

Although the carrier was not perfect, it was in much demand for a variety of roles in the British and Commonwealth forces. The British soon decided that it was too costly to continue building different versions of the carrier for each new role envisioned for it, and opted to build a basic vehicle that could be changed for different jobs by small modification kits installed at the factory. This new vehicle was now officially referred to as the Universal Carrier, although most soldiers continued to call it a Bren.

The Universal Carrier was built in Britain, Australia, New Zealand, Canada, and even in the United States. The US contractor, Ford Motor Co., found the vehicle to be underpowered and poorly designed for ease of production. In an attempt to improve the design, Ford developed a version known as the T16 carrier. The T16 was slightly longer and taller than the original Universal. Almost 14,000 T16s and an improved model known as the T16E2 were built by Ford between 1941 and 1945. The T16 series of vehicles never saw service with the US Army during WWII, with one exception: on December 12, 1941, a Canadian ship carrying fifty-seven carriers of the Canadian Army, was trapped by Japanese fleet movements in the Philippines. When Gen. Douglas MacArthur, US commander in

the Philippines, found out that the T16s were there, he asked the Canadian government for permission to use them in defense of the Philippines, as he now faced a Japanese invasion threat. As a result, forty of these Canadian carriers were supplied to two American National Guard tank units sent to the Philippines a month before. The remaining seventeen carriers were assigned to a Philippine Scout (Horse) unit for use with its scout-car section. No weapons were included with the T16s, so the Army equipped them all with American-made machine guns. Unfortunately for the Americans and Philippine soldiers, the overwhelming Japanese forces took control of the Philippines by April 9, 1942.

The T16 and Universal carriers saw widespread service during WWII and beyond. After WWII, Israel and other countries bought surplus carriers. Because of the vast amount built (almost 50,000), a number of T16 and Universal carriers can be found in the collectors' market. There at least 30 Bren-type carriers now in private hands. Prices for a hulk start at $5,000 and go up to $10,000 for an operational vehicle. A fully restored vehicle might sell for $18,000.

The various models of Bren-type carriers make great little armored vehicles for any collector. They are fast, fun to drive, and easy to

Designed for the British Army before WWII, the small open-topped Bren Gun Carrier saw widespread use during WWII. Used in many different roles, the Bren was not the perfect vehicle. An improved model known as the Universal Carrier was built in Britain, Australia, Canada, and New Zealand. Pictured is an early-model Bren and its combat team. *British Army*

The Soviet Army was supplied with several Universal carriers during WWII. This particular vehicle is carrying both a Bren light machine gun and a large .55cal Boys antitank rifle. *Armor magazine*

work on. Their suspension system tends to bounce you around on rough terrain, however—but that adds to the fun of driving them. Because of their small size and light weight they are a perfect vehicle for a collector that is pressed for space.

M39 APC

Near the end of WWII, the Army began developing a fully tracked APC. One of its first attempts involved taking the chassis of an M18 Hellcat tank destroyer, removing its turret, and replacing it with an open superstructure. This vehicle became known as the M39 utility vehicle and entered Army service in 1945. It was not widely used as an infantry transporter because the only way to enter or exit it was by climbing over its sides. In combat, this method of operation could be very dangerous when under fire. The open-topped superstructure also left the occupants very vulnerable to artillery fragments and small arms fire.

The M39 could reach a top speed of 65mph. Its hull was of welded-steel, no thicker than 1/4in. The driver and assistant driver sat at the front of the hull, and the transmission was located between them. The suspension system was of the torsion-bar type and consisted of five dual road wheels, on either side of the hull, each of which had a shock absorber. The drive sprocket was located at the front, with the idler at the rear. Four track return rollers were located on either side of the hull.

During the Korean War, its light weight and high horsepower made the M39 very adept in climbing some of the very steep hills that other vehicles couldn't climb. It became a very capable supply vehicle. Some units of the 2nd Infantry Division in Korea mounted 81mm mortars in their M39s.

Those M39s that survived combat were phased out of the Army inventory in 1957.

The M39 is fairly rare in collectors circles. Only one has been fully restored, and four others exist only as hulks. Many parts are very scarce, including the tracks. An M39 hulk will cost about $5,000, and an operational example may be $20,000. A fully restored vehicle would be worth $65,000 and up.

M75 APC

Another vehicle under development near the end of WWII was a fully tracked, completely armor-protected APC called the M44. The M44 consisted of a large, enclosed, box-like steel-armored superstructure that could carry at least twenty-five infantrymen plus the driver and vehicle commander, and was mounted on the chassis of the M18 tank destroyer. This time, the onboard troops could enter and exit through large rear access doors. While the overhead protection offered by this new vehicle was a big improvement over that of the open-topped half-tracks it was supposed to replace, the Army considered the vehicle too large because it didn't fit into its tactical (combat) doctrine, which stressed the ten-man squad as the basic building block of its infantry units. As a result, only a few M44s were built, some of which saw action during the later stages of the Korean War. An improved model of the M44, known as the M44E1, was fitted with roof hatches. The US Air Force (USAF) also used a few M44s as tactical-air-control vehicles.

By 1944, the Army realized that half-tracks were already obsolete and began developing a fully tracked armored utility vehicle known as the M39. Designed to carry cargo or troops, the M39 was open-topped. Getting in and out of it was not easy—as is dramatically shown here by members of an Army reconnaissance unit in 1953. *US Army*

The Army quickly began work on building a scaled-down version of the M44, known as the T18. Instead of twenty-seven men, the T18 could carry only twelve. After testing the T18, in 1952 it was ordered into production as the M75 APC. International Harvester Co. and FMC Corporation both built the vehicle, with a combined total of 1,729 M75s coming off the production lines between 1952 and 1954.

The M75 set the basic stage for a whole series of future Army APCs. Its arrangement—with the driver and engine in the front of the vehicle, the commander in the center behind the engine compartment, and the ten-man infantry squad in the rear compartment—was to be the same layout found in both the later M59 and M113 APCs.

The M75 was powered by a Continental six-cylinder gas engine that produced 295hp at 2,660rpm. It had a top speed of about 44mph and an operational range of about 115 miles. Its armor protection, like that of the M44 before it and the vehicles that followed it, ranged from 1/4in to 1in at the thickest point.

The M75 was not amphibious, and the engine air-cooling grilles on the sides of the hull were considered too vulnerable to small arms fire, so even as the M75 was just starting to be built, the Army began looking with great interest at an FMC design for a smaller and cheaper vehicle that was also fully amphibious. The resulting amphibious APC was accepted into Army service in 1953 as the M59.

The first fully tracked APC built for the Army that featured overhead armor protection was the M75. Seeing limited service in the Korean War, the M75 could carry twelve passengers. The Army thought it was too large and wanted it to be amphibious, and searched for better vehicles. Surplus M75s were supplied to the Belgium Army; after being replaced there, many came into private collectors' hands. *US Army*

This former-Belgium Army M75 APC belongs to a private collector and is waiting for the day that it can be restored to its original operational condition. *Michael Green*

As more M59s were built, the Army phased out of service all of its M75s, giving most of them to the Belgian Army, which used them until the early 1980s, when they were replaced by M113s. As the M75s were given under a military aid program, Belgium was required to return them to the US government when they were no longer needed. The obsolete M75s were sold as scrap to a number of dealers, but at least 25 M75s made it into private collections. At 18 tons the vehicle is fairly light when compared to many other AFVs, and parts and engines are not that difficult to find. It's an easy vehicle to work on. The entire engine slides out on rails for maintenance. Learning to drive it is also fairly easy. Prices for a hulk start at $5,000, with an operational vehicle going for $12,000 to $15,000. A restored vehicle can sell for $18,000 to $25,000.

M59 APC

The most common fully tracked APC now available to collectors is the American-designed-and-built M59. Almost 4,000 were produced by FMC Corporation between 1953 and 1959. Like its larger predecessor, the M75, the M59 was basically a large steel armored box on tracks, designed to carry at least ten infantrymen—but it was also fully amphibious, its tracks propelling it in the water. The driver

sat at the front and the commander sat or stood in the center of the hull; the commander had a cupola with periscopes. Earlier models had a pintle mount for the commander's .50cal Browning machine gun. Later-production models, known as the M59A1, were fitted with an enclosed, armored machine gun cupola for the .50cal machine gun.

The M59 was powered by two GM six-cylinder engines of 127hp each at 3,350rpm. The engines were mounted on either side of the hull, and each drove a track. The M59 could reach a top speed of 42mph and had an operating range of about 300 miles.

The M59 had a typical American torsion-bar suspension system, with five dual sets of road wheels on either side of the hull. The drive sprocket was at the front and the idler was at the rear. There were three track return rollers on either side of the vehicle.

Internal access was provided by a large hydraulically operated ramp in the rear hull. An armored door in the middle of the ramp was an emergency backup in case the ramp ever became jammed. There were also two hatches on top of the hull for the onboard troops to use if necessary.

As with most American APCs, the M59 was modified for a variety of different roles, including ambulance carrier, command and control vehicle, or weapons carrier. Because of a number of development problems, the only M59 variant built was the M84, which mounted a 4.2in mortar in its rear hull compartment.

While the M59 had some advantages over the M75, the Army was dissatisfied with the M59 in service use. The twin-engine combination was problematic and hard to maintain. The vehicle was underpowered and couldn't keep up with the Army tanks of the time. Its amphibious ability was also very poor by Army standards. The Army went back to FMC in 1955 with a request for a new APC that would correct all the shortcomings of the M59. The result was the M113 series of APCs.

As soon as the M113 became available in large numbers, the M59 was pulled out of service. Some M59s found their way to other countries, including Lebanon, Greece, and Brazil, but most were scrapped or used as hard targets on Army or USAF firing ranges. Approximately twenty-five M59s have survived long enough to pass into private hands. Engines for M59s are easy to find and fairly cheap. Prices start at $5,000 for a hulk, $15,000 for an operational model. A restored example can cost about $22,000.

M113 APC

Just coming into collectors' hands are a handful of the M113 series of vehicles. The M113 is one of the most widely used AFVs in the world today. Its familiar box-like shape can be seen in the United States and at least forty-four foreign countries. Almost 90,000 have been built since 1960 by FMC Corporation. Still in production, the M113 has been continually improved over the years to incorporate evolving vehicle technologies and remain a viable vehicle for military use.

When first built, the M113 was revolutionary because it was the first time that aluminum armor was used to provide a vehicle lightweight enough to be dropped by para-chute. FMC also pioneered the techniques that made aluminum welding feasible for mass production. The M113 chassis has been used as the foundation for an entire family of different vehicle types, including mortar carriers, unarmored cargo carriers, flamethrowers, command and control vehicles, antiaircraft gun and missile carriers, recovery vehicles, and fire support.

The typical twelve-ton M113 is configured as an APC for twelve infantrymen and a driver. It is capable of amphibious operations across lakes and streams, extended cross-country travel over rough terrain, and high-speed travel on improved roads and highways.

The aluminum armor, less than 1in thick, protects against shell fragments, flash burns, and small-arms fire only. The newest-model M113 can be fitted with add-on armor.

The original M113 was built with an industrial 209hp Chrysler 75M gas engine coupled

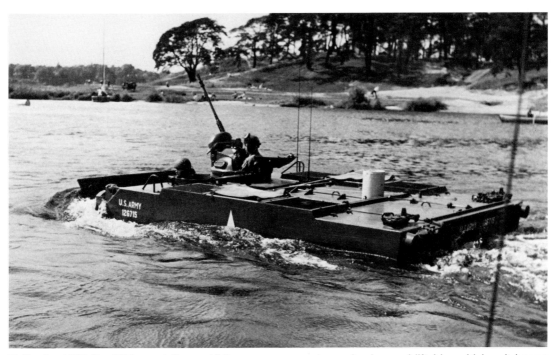

Unlike the M75, the M59 was fully amphibious, as this picture shows. Made of steel armor plate, the M59 was too heavy to be airlifted by cargo planes of the period. Since the Army was then placing much emphasis on airliftable vehicles, it began looking for a replacement for the M59. The vehicle chosen was the M113. *FMC Corporation*

To replace the M75, the Army fielded the M59 APC, capable of carrying a squad of eleven men plus the commander and driver. Unlike the M39 armored utility vehicle, where the passengers had to climb in or out of the vehicle, the M59 had a large rear door ramp that could be lowered for quick and easy access. *FMC Corporation*

to a commercial Allison TX200-2A transmission and an FMC D5200 controlled differential. The newest versions of the M113 are powered by a 275hp Detroit Diesel 6V53T engine.

Early M113s had a top speed of 40mph and a range of about 100 miles. The newest M113s can reach about 43mph and have a range of almost 300 miles. The M113 is equipped with a torsion-bar suspension system with ten individually sprung dual rubber-tired wheels. Due to suspension system improvements over the years, the M113 has gone from 3in of road-wheel travel up to 7in.

The M113 is basically a simple aluminum armor box with a sloped front on a fully tracked chassis. The driver and engine are located at the front of the vehicle, leaving most of the interior compartment free for personnel, cargo, or weapon systems. The commander sits or stands in the front center; his cupola is fitted with a number of vision blocks, and attached to a pintle mount is a .50cal Browning machine gun. When configured as an APC, the M113 carries a ten-man squad on bench seats and two jump seats located under the commander's cupola. A large, hydraulically operated ramp in the rear hull makes access easy. Within this large ramp is a separate armored door which can be opened when it is unnecessary to lower the entire rear ramp. On top of the box-like M113 hull is a large roof hatch that can be opened to allow some of the onboard troops to either exit the vehicle if needed or to fire weapons over its sides.

When the M113 entered into Army service, most of the US armored strength was in Western Europe facing the Soviet military threat. The M113 was seen as only a battlefield taxi, an AFV that could bring into combat a squad of infantrymen to support Army tanks. Since it was not designed as a fighting vehicle, the M113 had only one machine gun.

As it turned out, the first M113s entered combat in South Vietnam in 1961, not Western Europe. They were used by the South Vietnamese Army in the Mekong Delta area to counter the growing strength of the Vietcong. The South Vietnamese military commanders failed to use the M113 properly at first, but as their soldiers gained experience, they learned how to take advantage of the M113's outstanding mobility to go after the Vietcong no matter where they were hiding.

Against the wishes of their Army advisors, however, the South Vietnamese began to mount as many weapons as could be fitted to their M113s and use them almost like tanks. Since the M113 when originally designed did not offer any protection for its occupants when firing their weapons, the South Vietnamese Army quickly found out that their M113 personnel, especially the .50cal Browning machine gunner, suffered very high losses in combat. To help protect their M113 crews, the South Vietnamese military developed a number of armored gunshields fitted on top of the hull.

When the Army was first deployed in large numbers to South Vietnam in the late 1960s, it quickly saw the benefits of these shields and had some home-built for its own vehicles. Eventually, FMC built for the Army a standard gun shield kit. These kits could be installed on both M113 (gas-powered) and M113A1 (diesel-powered) APCs and on M125 (gas-powered, 81mm) or M106 (diesel-powered, 4.2in) mortar carriers. When added to the mortar carriers, only the commander's cupola was used.

Overall, the M113 was very successful in combat use during the Vietnam War, and after the war, its versatility and low cost appealed to many other countries, especially Germany, Israel, and Italy, who have approximately 5,000 each. Egypt, Australia, Belgium,

The overall shape of the M113 was very similar to that of the M59, but the M113 was smaller and lighter. To make it airliftable, the M113 was made out of aluminum armor. *FMC Corporation*

An interesting picture of the number of large parachutes needed to airdrop an M113. While this capability was an important design requirement for the M113, it was almost never used. *FMC Corporation*

Brazil, Canada, Denmark, Pakistan, Jordan, and Spain use varying numbers of the M113, ranging from a few dozen up to 1,000. Italy and Belgium also build their own M113s under license from FMC Corporation.

Considering the incredible numbers of M113 vehicles built and in use around the world, there are very few available for sale to collectors. The main problem is that the M113 remains a useful vehicle for armies everywhere. The only vehicles that have become available are a single FMC prototype M113 APC and a few Israeli Army M113 APCs that had been modified with added hull-mounted firing ports. In addition to the armored versions of the M113, a few unarmored M548 cargo carriers based on the M113 chassis are now for sale.

Prices for even an MII3 hulk start at $30,000. For an operational vehicle the price goes up to $40,000, and for a fully restored vehicle the price can go up to $60,000. Parts are very expensive since there is still a lot of demand for them.

British Saracen Wheeled APC

During WWII, the British Army used many American-built half-tracks to carry infantrymen into battle. Like the US Army, the British Army was not satisfied with the open-topped nature of the vehicle or its very poor cross-country mobility. After the war, the British began developing a new six-wheeled APC that became known as the Saracen.

The Saracen was rushed into production in 1952 to meet the needs of the British Army then involved in trying to suppress a communist uprising in Malaysia. It was later used in the British Army mechanized infantry battalions and reconnaissance regiments. The Saracen also proved to be quite marketable and was sold to a number of other countries, including Kuwait, Nigeria, Australia, and Jordan.

Built by Alvis Ltd. of Coventry, England, until 1979, the Saracen was nothing more than an armored box on wheels. The Saracen's Rolls-Royce engine produced 160hp at 3,750rpm. Top speed was about 45mph and operational range was approximately 250 miles.

With a thin, welded-steel armored hull, the Saracen could carry ten infantrymen plus the driver and commander. The driver sat behind the engine in the crew compartment; his armored hatch was fitted with three periscopes for use during combat but it could be folded forward for better visibility at other times. The vehicle commander sat in a small, armored turret on the forward port of the hull. The turret was fitted with a .30cal Browning machine gun and could be turned 360deg by hand. The top of the turret could be folded forward, with the rear part of the turret folded down to provide a crude seat for the commander. The Saracen could carry 3,000 rounds of ammunition for the machine gun. The onboard troops could also fire their own small arms through three firing ports in each side of the hull.

The Saracen's advanced mobility (for its day) was accomplished with a fully independent double wishbone suspension system fitted with torsion bars and sleeves. Two telescopic double-acting hydraulic-operated shock absorbers were fitted to the front and rear wheels. The center wheels had only a single shock absorber.

The first postwar APC produced for the British Army was the six-wheeled Saracen. Production began in 1952. The Saracen was a popular vehicle and was widely sold to several foreign armies. Constructed of thin steel armor, it could carry a crew of two, plus ten passengers. *Armor magazine*

The M113 was basically a very simple armored box on tracks. The driver and engine were at the front of the hull, leaving the rest of the hull compartment free to carry troops or cargo. The onboard troops entered or exited the vehicle by a large rear door ramp. *FMC Corporation*

The Saracen was steered with the front four wheels which were connected by a mechanical linkage hydraulically assisted between the steering wheel and the road wheels. There were hydraulic brakes on each wheel. If the Saracen lost its front wheels because of an antitank mine, it could continue to operate for a period of time until repair could be made.

The Saracen was designed by the British at the same time as the Saladin armored car, which was armed with a 76.2mm cannon. Both the Saladin and Saracen were based on the same six-wheeled chassis, but due to different roles, each had a completely different hull and turret arrangement. The Saracen went into production first because the British Army thought it needed a fast-moving APC

more than an armored car with a large cannon.

In British Army service, the Saracen was replaced beginning in the early 1960s with a fully tracked APC known as the FV432. That held true in other countries' armies also, and the Saracen was slowly replaced as more modern vehicles became available. Many smaller countries continue to use the Saracen in police-type duties.

For American AFV collectors accustomed to working on the fairly simple and straightforward automotive components of US-built vehicles, the Saracen is a very interesting historical vehicle to work on. Like British cars, British AFVs tend to be much more complex than similar US-built vehicles.

A big problem with the Saracen is the price

One of the few M113s to find itself in private collectors' hands is this vehicle, which included several hull-mounted firing ports. A few M113s so modified were sold to Israel, which later released them for sale. *Jacques Littlefield*

of spare parts which tend to be expensive. Another serious problem concerns the vehicle's transmission. If it is not used properly, you can blow the seals in it very easily. To replace the transmission you would have to pull the engine out, which is a real pain.

An operational Saracen will fetch at least $18,000. A fully restored vehicle may go for $28,000. There are about thirty such vehicles in private hands.

British FV1611 Humber Pig

During the mid-1950s, the British Army was very short of APCs. The Saracen was a fine vehicle, but not enough of them were being built to fulfill British Army requirements. Fully tracked APCs were not yet even on the drawing boards. As an interim measure, the British Army took a four-wheel-drive truck, developed in the late 1940s and early 1950s, and modified its chassis to mount a box-like steel armored hull. This vehicle became the FV1611 Humber; more than 1,700 were built between 1955 and 1959. The chassis for the Humber were built by the English Co. Humber/Rootes, and the armored bodies were built by the Royal Ordnance Factory at Woolwich and GkN Sankey.

The Humber could carry eight infantrymen plus a driver and commander. The box-like structure of the hull was ballistically very poorly shaped and afforded protection against some types of small-arms fire only.

For the eight infantrymen sitting in the rear compartment, there were two firing ports on either side of the hull. The Humber had no armament of its own. Two twin rear doors with single firing ports installed in them provided access.

Powered by a Rolls-Royce gas engine of 120hp at 3,750rpm, the Humber had a top speed of about 40mph and an operational range of 250 miles. It had a torsion-bar type suspension system with hydraulic shock absorbers fitted to each wheel. Because the heavy weight of its armored body tended to bottom out the suspension system, the British soldiers who used it nicknamed it the "Pig."

Other versions of the Humber included an ambulance, command and control vehicle, load carrier, towing vehicle for a mortar-locating radar system, and an antitank missile-launching version known as the Hornet.

In the early 1960s, as increasing numbers of Saracen APCs and the newer fully tracked FV432 APC entered British Army service, the Humbers were sold as scrap in England and overseas.

In the meantime, Northern Ireland was experiencing intensified troubles between the

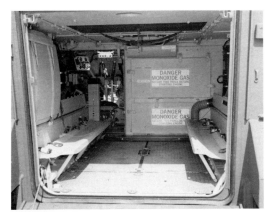

An interior photo of an M113 APC. The driver's position was on the left, and the engine compartment was on the right. Two bench seats folded down to accommodate ten men (five on either side). Behind the bench seats on the left was the fuel tank. *FMC Corporation*

Because the crew and passengers in the M113 had to expose the upper parts of their bodies to fire their weapons, an arrangement of armored shields was built as added protection. Pictured is an American-designed-and-built kit fitted to an M113. *FMC Corporation*

different religious groups, and the British Army found itself stationed in greater numbers there to act as a buffer between the warring sides. It was quickly realized that the Humber would be the perfect patrol vehicle for the Northern Ireland cities and towns. As a result, the British government went back to all the scrap dealers it had originally sold the surplus Humbers to and repurchased them. The government impounded those vehicles that had been acquired by collectors.

By the early 1970s, the British were forced to up-armor the Humbers since the Irish Republican Army began using high-velocity small arms ammunition. In addition to extra armor, vision blocks were fitted to the hull firing ports. A number of Humbers were also fitted with tear gas launchers to help disperse crowds.

At the moment, there are approximately twenty-four Humbers still in private hands. There are none in the US. Prices for the Humber are fairly cheap, with $5,000 getting you an operational vehicle. A fully restored example might cost $10,000.

Soviet BTR-152 Wheeled APC

After WWII, the Soviets developed a number of wheeled armored transport vehicles, one of the most common of which was the

BTR-152. First developed in 1946, it didn't go into full-scale production until 1950. Based on the chassis of a 6x6 two-ton military cargo truck, the BTR-152 was nothing more than a lightly armored steel hull mounted on a truck chassis. It was open-topped, making those inside very vulnerable to artillery and mortar fire, but it was cheap and easy to build in large numbers. Completely obsolete by modern standards, the BTR-152 still soldiers on in numerous Third World countries, where its very simple and crude design is an asset.

The general outline of the BTR-152 looks vaguely like the American and German halftracks of WWII, but without the rear tracks of the half-tracks, its cross-country mobility suf-

fers in comparison. To improve its mobility, early versions of the BTR-152 had an external tire pressure regulation system that allowed the driver to alter the amount of air within its six large, truck-type tires. The BTR-152 was usually armed with only one machine gun, and like most Soviet APCs, it had hull-mounted firing ports.

Powered by a six-cylinder gas engine, the BTR-152 had a top speed of about 46mph. It could carry a two-man crew, plus fourteen infantrymen up to 400 miles. Some versions were fitted with overhead armored covers, and infrared driving lights were added to most BTR-152s later. At least one version of the BTR-152 was modified to carry a twin-

Besides use as an APC, the Saracen was modified with a raised hull, enabling it to serve as a command-and-control vehicle. There was also an am-

bulance version of the Saracen built in small numbers. *Armor magazine*

The BTR-40 was the second APC to enter Soviet military service after WWII. First built in 1950, the BTR-40 was nothing more than a four-wheel truck chassis fitted with an armored body. It was open-topped and had very thin armor protection, and the Soviet military quickly developed better vehicles that rendered the BTR-40 obsolete. It is still used in some Third World armies. The vehicle pictured belongs to a private collector. *Michael Green*

The first APC to enter Soviet military service after WWII was the BTR-152. Based on the chassis of a six-wheel-drive truck, the BTR-152 was fitted with a thin armored hull. No longer in front-line service with the Soviet armies, the BTR-152 can be found in the service of many Third World armies. *Greg Stewart*

The BTR-152 driver sits on the left of the vehicle with the commander to his right. There is a small armored roof over the driver's and commander's seats. There was no protection for the seventeen soldiers in the rear of the troop compartment. The vehicle pictured is a modified command post version of the BTR-152 with an overhead cover. *Michael Green*

barreled 14.5mm heavy antiaircraft machine gun.

Many of the BTR-152s supplied to various Arab armies over the years have been captured by the Israeli Army, some of which were used by the Israeli Border Patrol.

BTR-152s are reasonably cheap by collectors' standards, and plenty are available. However, the vehicles lack the appeal of better-known vehicles.

Operational BTR-152s sell for about $15,000. A fully restored vehicle might cost $30,000. At the moment there are three BTR-152s in private hands. The biggest problem with such ex-Soviet vehicles is the lack of a dependable source of spare parts.

Soviet BTR-40 APC

Entering service in 1951, the BTR-40 APC was nothing more than a short-wheelbase version of a four-wheel-drive Soviet truck known as the GAZ-63 fitted with an armored body. In addition to a commander and driver, the BTR-40 could carry eight infantrymen. There were firing ports in the hull for the

In the early 1950s, the British military modified a 1-ton four-wheel-drive truck with an armored body. Known as the Humber armored truck, this vehicle was used as a makeshift APC until more Saracens could be fielded. Because of its poor riding ability, the vehicle was nicknamed the "Pig" by British soldiers. *Chris Foss*

troops to use their own personnel weapons. Normally, there was a 7.62mm machine gun pintle mounted forward in the troop compartment.

The BTR-40 was powered by a six-cylinder gas engine producing 80hp at 3400rpm. It had a top speed on paved roads of about 50mph and an operational range of about 250 miles.

Like most Soviet military vehicles, the BTR-40 chassis was used for several roles, including an antiaircraft vehicle fitted with twin 14.5mm machine guns and a special chemical reconnaissance decontamination vehicle.

Long since replaced in Soviet military service, the BTR-40 was given to a large number of Third World countries, where some still serve.

Hungarian PSZH-IV APC

Looking much like a Soviet-built BRDM-2 scout car (described in the next chapter), the Hungarian military considers its PSZH-IV an APC. It has the same armament as the BRDM-2 but in a slightly different turret. The PSZH-IV has a crew of three—a commander, gun-

An interior photo of the BTR-40 shows the driver's compartment. The vehicle was powered by a six-cylinder, water-cooled, gas engine. Early-production vehicles had no firing ports, but later-production vehicles had two or three on each side of the hull. *Michael Green*

ner, and driver—plus seats for an additional five soldiers. It is 19ft 1in tall, 7ft 6in wide, and 8ft 3in tall.

Like most vehicles of its class and size, the PSZH-IV is protected by steel armor less than 1in thick, which provides protection from small arms fire only. Because of its role as an APC, the PSZH-IV has doors on either side of the hull. The vehicle commander and driver also have hatches above their positions.

The PSZH-IV is fully amphibious, pro-pelled in the water by two water jets in the rear hulls, and is fitted with several infrared night-vision devices. It is powered by a six-cylinder, 160hp diesel engine, which gives it a top speed of 62mph and an operational range of 310 miles.

The turret is fitted with two machine guns: a 14.5mm and a 7.62mm. It is traversed by hand. There are also two firing ports on each side of the hull so that the on-board troops can use their own firearms if needed.

Belonging to a private collector is this Hungarian Army PSZH-IV APC. With a crew of three, the vehicle could carry six additional passengers. The small turret of the PSZH-IV was fitted with a 14.5mm machine gun and a 7.62mm machine gun. *Michael Green*

Hungary has sold the PSZH-IV to Bulgaria, Czechoslovakia, East Germany, Iran, and Iraq for use in their armies.

For a collector, the PSZH-IV is a fairly comfortable vehicle to drive because all the driving controls are boosted. At the moment, there are only about five of these vehicles in private hands. Unfortunately, the vehicles brought out of Hungary for collectors tend to be a little rough around the edges. An operational vehicle goes for about $25,000. A restored vehicle done outside of Hungary would cost an extra $5,000.

Chapter 5

Armored Reconnaissance Vehicles

Pictured on parade in Berlin, before WWII, are these light four-wheel-drive Sdkfz 221 armored cars. Originally armed with only a machine gun in a small open-topped turret, later models carried a variety of weapons, including a 20mm cannon. *Armor magazine*

This prewar picture shows a German Army Sdkfz 221 armored car during a training exercise. The vehicle itself was fitted with a wrap-around frame antennae. The Sdkfz 221 series of armored cars had a crew of two and were powered by an eight-cylinder gas engine. *National Archives*

German Sdkfz 221 and Sdkfz 222 ARVs

The German Army had very little interest in tanks for most of World War I. It wasn't until near the end of the war that the Germans tried to build approximately a dozen of their own tanks. They also used captured British and French tanks. But it was a story of too little too late. After World War I ended, the Western Allies imposed upon the Germans several treaties, one of which banned military equipment, including tanks. The Germans could have only a few armored cars for police purposes.

It wasn't until Hitler came to power and began the rearmament of the German military in 1935 that armored cars began to be built in large numbers. They ranged from specially designed eight-wheeled armored cars to six-wheel types and finally the smaller four-wheeled armored cars based on the chassis of a heavy passenger car.

Of the many thousands of armored cars used by the Germans during WWII, only a handful of the smaller four-wheeled versions have survived long enough to pass into collectors' hands.

Known as the Sdkfz 221/222 light armored car series, these rear-engined vehicles had all-wheel-drive, a fully independent suspension system with dual coil springs, and self-locking differentials.

The typical Sdkfz 221/222 was 15ft 9in long, 6ft 5in wide, and 5ft 7in tall, and weighed 4–5 tons. The welded-steel hull and turret were protection against small arms fire only. The open-topped turret was covered by a hinged wire-mesh screen designed to keep out hand grenades. There was a door on either side of the hull, as well as a number of hinged, armored visors on both the front and rear of the vehicle.

Early models of the Sdkfz 221 were armed with only one machine gun. In an effort to upgrade their firepower, a few vehicles were modified to mount a 20mm tapered-bore anti-tank gun.

The Sdkfz 222 was an improved version of the Sdkfz 221. With an eight-cylinder gas engine, the Sdkfz 222 had a top speed of about 50mph and an operational range of 150 miles. The Sdkfz 222 had a larger turret than the

Throughout the 1930s, the Army experimented with a variety of modified civilian armored cars. It wasn't until shortly before WWII that the Army finally got a purposely built armored car with four-wheel-drive. Known as the M3A1 scout car, it was open-topped and armed with a variety of machine guns. *National Archives*

An overview of an M3A1 scout car in Army service shows the skate rail around the hull, which allowed the vehicle's weapons to be quickly slid around to any position. While a number of M3A1 scout cars have survived to pass into private collections, certain parts, such as the skate rail, have long ago been cut off and thrown away. *National Archives*

Sdkfz 221 and mounted a 20mm automatic gun adapted from an aircraft weapon, which had a ten-shot magazine and could fire armor-piercing or high-explosive rounds. Mounted alongside the 20mm gun was an MG34 machine gun. The vehicle had a three-man crew.

When used during the German invasion of Poland and France, these armored cars performed very well. So successful were these vehicles that both the British and US armies began to develop their own versions.

The Sdkfz 221/222 light armored cars proved to be completely overwhelmed by the very severe terrain and weather on the Russian Front. With very long lines of resupply, the Germans found their four-wheeled light armored cars very difficult to maintain in the field for long periods of time.

In 1942, the Germans canceled production of all four-wheeled light armored cars in favor of the larger eight-wheeled armored cars. On the Russian Front, the German Army tended to replace its wheeled armored cars with small half-tracks fitted with the guns and turret of the Sdkfz 222 armored car.

There were other variations of the Sdkfz 221/222, each with its own designation. Most of them were outfitted with different combinations of radio gear and served as command and control vehicles.

All German WWII AFVs are extremely rare and command top dollar on the collectors' market. There are only two Sdkfz 222 armored cars now in private hands. The chance others will show up is extremely rare. As a result, these vehicles would bring at least $50,000 for a hulk.

US M3A1 Scout Car

As early as 1916, the Army had begun using small numbers of commercial automobiles as scouts. This policy continued until the 1930s, when discussions turned toward specialized, wheeled scout vehicles with armor protection and better off-road mobility than the two-wheel-drive civilian vehicles. It wasn't until 1934 that the Indiana Motortruck Co., a subsidiary of White Motor Co., developed the first true scout car designed from the ground up. Based on a four-wheel-drive truck chassis, the vehicle was known as the Scout Car T7, or M1. It eventually evolved into the White Motor Co. M3A1 scout car in 1939, almost 20,000 of which were built between 1940 and early 1944.

In its final form, the vehicle was equipped with a JXD Hercules six-cylinder, in-line, gas engine which gave it a top speed of 55mph and an operational range of about 250 miles. The same JXD Hercules engine was used in the Army's M8/20 six-wheeled armored cars. Coupled to the M3A1's engine was a four-speed "crash box" (non-synchromesh).

The armor hull of the open-topped M3A1 scout car consisted of 1/4in flat-steel armor plates. Top and side protection for the front-mounted engine was provided by an armored hood. During combat, armored shutters, controlled by the driver, could be closed to protect the radiator.

The driver and commander sat in the front, and six scouts could ride in the rear hull compartment. Armament normally consisted of a .50cal and .30cal machine gun.

The windshield was of shatterproof glass.

Belonging to a private collector, this M3A1 scout car shows the front-mounted roller, which was supposed to assist the vehicle when crossing steep embankments. In practice, this feature was almost completely useless. *Michael Green*

In action, a 1/2in armored plate could be lowered over the glass. The armored plate had two direct vision slots to allow the driver to see where he was going. There were also hinged armored plate upper doors that could be swung into position if needed.

The M3A1 scout car weighed about 5 tons, and was 18ft 5-1/2in long, 6ft 8in wide, and 6ft 6-1/2in tall.

At the front of the M3A1 was a roller assembly designed to keep the vehicle from impaling itself at the bottoms of steep embankments or deep ditches. In theory, this spring-loaded caster/roller was supposed to either turn or travel upwards and back against its springs when sufficient pressure was applied. In actual practice, it didn't do much good at all. But it was continued in production on both the M3A1 scout car and many White Motor Co. half-track models. Later-production half-tracks were fitted with a much more useful and practical front-mounted winch as a replacement.

Because the M3A1 scout car looked very similar to the American-built WWII-era half-tracks, many people mistakenly think that the two vehicles shared parts. This is not true. All the major drive line and mechanical components were very different; even most of the external items on the vehicles, such as doors and fenders, were different and would not interchange.

Almost half of the 20,000 M3A1 scout cars built were shipped to the USSR. Others were used by other Allied armies, such as the British and Free French. The Army, USMC, and Army Air Corps also used a few as utility vehicles.

Due to the nature of its design, the M3A1 had very poor off-road mobility. The Army considered the vehicle obsolete very early in WWII. As more half-tracks and M8 or M20 armored cars came into the Army inventory, those M3A1s not given away were pushed into noncombat support roles.

After WWII, the Army finally got rid of all its scout cars. However, other postwar armies continued to find the M3A1 scout car a useful vehicle until fielding newer generations of their own wheeled scout vehicles. The M3A1 scout car can still be found in use with Third World military police units.

The best-known British-built armored car of WWII was the small four-wheel Daimler Dingo. Powered by a rear-mounted engine, the Dingo had a two-man crew. The vehicle pictured belongs to a private collector. *Richard Bryd*

In the United States, M3A1 scout cars were sold as surplus to the civilian market as late as the 1950s. Many were bought by local government agencies for a variety of uses, from snowplows to boxcar pushers. This means that the armor has been removed on many surviving M3A1 scout cars, and since parts are very hard to find for these vehicles, it becomes difficult to restore them to their original condition. Complete original M3A12 scout cars are, therefore, fairly rare and fetch a handsome price.

There are approximately 45 M3A1 scout cars in private hands at the moment. A hulk can be had for $10,000 with an operational vehicle going for $15,000. A fully restored scout car can sell for up to $25,000. Being completely street legal, the M3A1 can be driven almost anywhere. Because they are underpowered, owners of this vehicle need to be very careful on freeways or going up hills. Another problem for collectors who wish to drive their vehicles around town are weak brakes.

British Daimler Dingo and Ford Lynx Light Armored Cars

In the years before WWII, the British Army had very little interest in wheeled armored cars, considering tracked AFVs superior. Successful German Army use of armored cars during the early stages of WWII, however, convinced the British to take another look at them.

With new-found interest, the British began to use a wide variety of wheeled armored cars of all types and sizes. The best-known vehicle of the time and now very popular among collectors is the Daimler Dingo light armored car. This was a small, four-wheel-drive, turretless, two-man vehicle that weighed fewer than 4 tons, and was only 4ft 11in tall, 10ft 5in long, and only 5ft 7in wide. Originally developed by Daimler Motors (BSA) as a liaison vehicle for British tank units, the Dingo had an independent coil-spring suspension system. The drive to the wheels was from a single central differential through side shafts, allowing the vehicle's rear-mounted engine and the drive to be located much lower in the hull.

Both the commander and driver sat in an octagonal armored crew compartment. The armor was thin and provided protection against some types of small arms fire only. A folding armored top provided some overhead protection for the crew compartment. Normally, the only armament the vehicle had was a Bren machine gun operated by the commander, which could be fired through a slot in the front hull plate.

The Dingo was powered by a Daimler six-cylinder gas engine which gave it a top speed of 55mph and an operational range of about 200 miles. The Dingo could also be driven backwards at very high speeds, a very popular feature among British scout crews, who often had to leave an area very quickly when spotted by the enemy.

Coming in five different models, a total of 6,626 Dingos were produced during WWII. It saw action around the globe with both British and Commonwealth military units, and con-

During WWII, the Canadian arms industry built a broadly based copy of the British-designed Daimler Dingo. Known as the Lynx scout car Mk. II, some of these vehicles lasted long enough to be used during the Vietnam War. The South Vietnamese Army Lynx pictured was bought from Malaysia, where it had been fitted with a makeshift machine gun turret. *National Archives*

M8 armored cars are very popular with collectors, since they can be made street-legal with certain modifications. The vehicle pictured belongs to a pri- vate collector and has been restored to near-mint condition. *Michael Green*

tinued to serve the British Army for many years after the war until replaced by the Ferret light armored car.

A Canadian armored car built during WWII broadly resembled the Dingo and was known as the Lynx scout car Mk. II. It is also available on the collectors' market, in fact for a little less than the Dingo. The Lynx was based on a special Ford chassis equipped with a hull built by International Harvester. Between 1942 and 1945, 3,255 were built. Like the Dingo, the Lynx continued to serve the Canadian Army after WWII. Both the Dingo and Lynx were used during the Korean War by United Nations forces and then were passed on to Third World armies. At least one Canadian Ford Lynx was used by the South Vietnamese Army for a time. Like all older generation AFVs, they eventually wear out, or the lack of spare parts forces them into the scrap pile.

Considering how many Dingos and Lynxs were built during WWII, very few have survived long enough to pass into collectors' hands. At the most, only four Dingos are in private hands, while only two Lynxs are in collections. Because of their rarity, some parts are very hard to find. The vehicles themselves start at $2,000 for a hulk, $15,000 for an operational vehicle, and up to $25,000 for a fully restored model.

US M8 and M20 Light Armored Cars

The US Army had experimented with a dazzling array of different types of armored cars since 1916 (most based on modified civilian trucks), but when WWII began in 1939, tanks, with their better off-road mobility, captured the attention and funding. Nevertheless, German military use of wheeled armored cars in the early stages of WWII persuaded the Army that it also needed a fast, lightweight armored car that could perform scouting and security duties.

The Army chose as its new armored car a Ford Motor Co. vehicle known as the T22, originally designed as a six-wheeled tank destroyer armed with a 37mm gun. Combat reports showed that the 37mm gun on the T22 was obsolete against German tanks, and since the T22 couldn't fulfill one role, the Army decided that it could prove more useful in another role. It was therefore reclassified as the M8 light armored car in June 1942 and was rushed into immediate production. In April 1943, a turretless version of the same vehicle was standardized as the M20 armored utility car and was used not only in the scouting role but also as a cargo carrier, command vehicle, or even as an APC.

During WWII, Ford Motor Co. built 8,523 M8s and 3,791 M20s. While the M8 was fitted with a turret mounting both a 37mm gun and a coaxial .30cal machine gun, the M20's armament was limited to a single .50cal machine gun mounted to an antiaircraft ring. Some M20s had a .30cal machine gun fitted instead of the standard .50cal machine gun.

Both the M20 and the M8 armored cars were 16ft 5in long and 8ft 4in wide. The M20 was slightly taller, at 7ft 7in, due to the installation of the .50cal machine gun ring mount. Each M20 had a two-man crew and seating for four passengers. The M8 could not carry

Originally designed as a tank destroyer, the Army's M8 armored car saw widespread service throughout the later stages of WWII. Never a big fan of armored cars, the Army considered the M8 under-gunned and lacking sufficient cross-country mobility. Dropped from the Army's inventory shortly after the Korean War, the M8 still sees service in some Third World armies. *US Army*

cargo or passengers, but had a four-man crew: The driver and assistant driver sat in the front hull, while the gunner and commander, who also acted as the loader, sat in the open-topped turret. The armor was thin and provided protection against small-arms fire only.

Both the M20 and M8 were powered by a rear-mounted Hercules six-cylinder, water-cooled gas engine, which gave a top speed of 56mph and an operational range of almost 270 miles. The M20 and M8 weighed 7–8 tons.

The M20s and M8s rode on six large wheels, two of which were attached to axles near the rear, while the third pair of wheels stabilized the front end. All of the wheels were powered, and semi-elliptical springs furnished the suspension system for its axles. The M20 and M8 could climb a 30deg slope, ford water up to 32in, and cross a 12in obstacle. Ground pressure was approximately 10-1/2lb per square inch, giving the vehicles excellent off-road mobility compared to that of other vehicles of the same weight class.

In British military service, the M8 was nicknamed the "Greyhound" because of its speed. While speed is always important to scout vehicles, sometimes such vehicles needed to fight their way into and out of situations. The Army concluded at the end of WWII that the M20 and M8 lacked sufficient firepower and armor protection to perform many of their as-

Based on the chassis of the M8 armored car was the M20 armored utility car. Designed to carry a crew or cargo, the M20 was simply an M8 without a turret. Instead, an open-topped compartment was built. The vehicle was armed with a .50cal machine gun mounted on a ring mount. The M20 pictured is being used by Army military police to guard enemy prisoners during the Korean War. *US Army*

Built for the British Army under contract in the United States, the T17E Staghound armored car was a four-wheel-drive vehicle armed originally with a 37mm cannon. Later models were modified by the British military to mount a variety of weapons. *US Army*

signed missions. As a result, the Army gradually began to phase out its inventory of M20 and M8 armored cars. The Korean War, which started in 1950, proved to be a reprieve, and many of these vehicles served throughout that conflict. After the Korean War, some of the remaining M20s and M8s were passed on to National Guard units, and by the time of the Vietnam War, they had disappeared from American military service. However, many European and Third World countries used them for many decades. Almost fifty years later, they can still be found in use in Greece, Columbia, and the Senegal. In the United States, several M20s and M8s are still used by police departments as riot control vehicles. The Los Angeles Police Department, for example, has an M20 with a large battering ram attached to its front to knock down the doors of barricaded crack houses.

A very popular AFV among collectors, the M8 and M20 are good starter vehicles because of their fairly simple design and layout. There are lots of spare parts around at very reasonable prices. Because it is a well-known vehicle, a beginner would have a lot of experience to draw upon when attempting to rebuild and operate his vehicle. A disadvantage with the M8 and M20 is their three-axle layout, which in some states requires a special operator's license.

There are sixty-seventy M8s and M20s in private hands. Prices for a hulk start at $15,000, with an operational vehicle going for $30,000. A fully restored vehicle would cost about $40,000.

British Staghound Armored Car

British factories could never build enough military vehicles (be they armored or not) during WWII to fulfill the requirements of its army. As a result, the British government contracted with American and Canadian companies to build vehicles for them. One of these vehicles was known as the Staghound armored car. Much like the British-built AEC armored car, the Staghound was designed for combat in North Africa. Unfortunately, by the time it reached production, fighting in North Africa was over. Instead, the Staghound saw combat in Western Europe, where the terrain was much better suited to the tank than to a heavily armored wheeled vehicle.

The Staghound was designed by the British and American armies together and built by Chevrolet. Production began in mid-1942 and ended in December 1943, with 3,900 vehicles built.

Weighing approximately 14 tons, it was patterned after American light tanks, but instead of tracks, it ran on four huge tires. It was powered by two GMC six-cylinder gas engines, which gave it a top speed of almost 60mph and an operational range of about 450 miles. The Staghound was 8ft 10in long, 7ft 9in wide, and 7ft 9in tall, and had a crew of five. The turret was made of cast-steel armor and mounted a 37mm gun and a coaxial .30cal machine gun. There was also another .30cal machine gun in the front hull. Later models were also fitted with a .30cal machine gun on the roof of the turret.

Like most AFVs, there were a number of different versions built. One model mounted a British-designed antiaircraft turret fitted with twin .50cal machine guns.

After WWII, many surplus Staghounds were supplied to NATO nations, especially Belgium, Denmark, and the Netherlands. Some of these vehicles survived in service until the 1960s. Many other Staghounds found their way to the Middle East and surrounding countries. As newer generations of armored cars were produced, most Staghounds eventually wore out and were scrapped by their owners. Only three

Belonging to a private collector, this beautifully restored M20 armored car is being displayed at Aberdeen Proving Grounds, Maryland, during its annual Armed Forces Day activities. *Michael Green*

Staghounds are currently in collectors' hands.

Prices start at $20,000 for a Staghound hulk and go up to $40,000 for an operational vehicle. A fully restored vehicle could be worth up to $60,000. While engines can be found for the Staghound, many other smaller parts can be extremely hard to find.

British Ferret Armored Car

Developed shortly after WWII, the size of the British-built Ferret armored car makes it very popular among collectors. Only 6ft 2in tall, 11ft 1in long, and 6ft 3in wide, the Ferret can fit into a collector's home garage. It has even been called "cute."

Between 1952 and 1971, Daimler Motors Co. of Coventry, England, built 4,409 Ferrets. Coming in a variety of variations, the Ferret was bought by more than thirty-five countries around the world. Still in limited service with the British military, the Ferret saw action with the British Army during Operation Desert Storm.

In its original form, the Ferret was an open-topped scout car with a three-man crew and armed only with a light machine gun. Later models were fitted with a one-man, manually operated turret mounting a single .30cal

Later models of the British Army Ferret scout car were fitted with a small, hand-operated, machine gun turret. The Ferret enjoyed widespread sales success with a large number of foreign armies. It still serves in numerous countries. *Armor magazine*

Shortly after WWII, the British Army developed the Ferret Mk. I scout car to replace the wartime Daimler Dingo scout car. Looking much like its predecessor in general outline, the Ferret had no turret fitted when originally designed. *Armor magazine*

Browning machine gun. The turret could be traversed by hand through a full circle. With the turret, the Ferret crew was reduced to two. Some later models were fitted with wire-guided antitank rockets.

The Ferret was of welded-steel-armor construction, the armor itself no thicker than 1/2in anywhere. The driver sat in the front hull and used an inverted steering wheel. The commander stood in the center of the vehicle, normally with his head outside of the turret for better vision. The standard Ferret weighed about 4 tons.

The Ferret was powered by a six-cylinder Rolls-Royce gas engine that gave it an operational range of a little under 200 miles and a top speed of almost 60mph.

As with any specially built military scout car, the Ferret featured four-wheel-drive, the run-flat wheels themselves are mounted on fully independent coil springs with wishbone linkages.

Being an older generation vehicle, the Ferret did not feature any type of night-vision devices. In its normal configuration, the Ferret was not amphibious, but when fitted with a collapsible flotation screen could cross calm, inland waters.

Because of its age and lack of more advanced features compared to those of other scout vehicles now in service, most Ferrets have been downgraded to internal security or police duties in many Third World countries. England, Canada, and New Zealand have removed Ferrets from their military inventories.

At the moment, an operational Ferret can be had for as little as $10,000. A fully restored model may cost $18,000. There are at least fifty or more Ferrets now in private hands. Engines and parts are available at fairly reasonable cost. Like most British AFVs, there are certain automotive design features that may seem odd for an American collector. Peter Wong, a Ferret owner, found that his ex-

perience working on Jaguar sport cars was a good background for rebuilding his Ferret.

British Saladin Armored Car

Designed and built around the same time as the Ferret, the Saladin can be considered a heavy armored car. Weighing 10 tons, it had a three-man crew and was armed with a 76.2mm medium-velocity cannon and a coaxial .30cal Browning machine gun.

The Saladin had six wheels, three evenly spaced on each side of the hull. All wheels were driven and the front four were steered. Its suspension was fully independent, fitted with torsion bars and sleeves, plus double-

The Ferret scout car was crewed by two men. The driver sat in the front hull and had several vision ports and periscopes. The vehicle commander, who sat in the one-man turret, operated the Ferret's single .30cal machine gun. *Armor magazine*

129

acting hydraulic shock absorbers. Disc brakes were fitted on each of the six wheels.

The driver sat in the front of the steel-armored hull and controlled the vehicle with an inverted power-assisted steering wheel. The commander and gunner rode in the turret, which could be turned 360deg by an electric motor; in case of a motor failure, the turret could be traversed manually. The Saladin could carry forty-three rounds of 76.2mm cannon rounds and 2,750 rounds of .30cal machine gun ammunition. It was powered by an eight-cylinder Rolls-Royce gas engine, giving it a top speed of about 45mph and an operational range of about 250 miles. The engine was connected to a Daimler fluid coupling which itself was connected to a Daimler gearbox of five gears in both forward and reverse.

The first Saladin was produced in 1959 and was built by Alvis Ltd. of Coventry, England. Production ended in 1972, with 1,177 vehicles built. The Saladin was sold to many countries in the early 1960s. West Germany bought ninety-seven Saladins for use by its Border Police and then later passed them on to Sudan. Jordan, which has always had a strong tradition of British military training and equipment, still uses the Saladin in police service.

The British Army long ago replaced its supply of Saladins with newer generation vehicles. The Australian Army, which had bought a number of Saladins in the 1960s, was unhappy with their limited mobility. When they were taken out of service, the Australian Army took the 76mm gun-armed turrets and mounted them on American-supplied M113 APCs. Somewhat top-heavy, these strange-looking vehicles were called M113A1 fire-support vehicles. A few were sent to South Vietnam in the late 1960s as part of the Australian contribution to the war effort, but they were not successful and were withdrawn.

The Saladin is a most impressive-looking AFV. It can also be made street legal without too much trouble. It is a fairly simple vehicle in layout and reflects the period in which it was built. Like the Saracen, from which it shares the same automotive components, the complex nature of the vehicle's drivetrain and suspension system can be a problem for a collector not already familiar with British AFV technology.

There are about ten Saladins currently in private hands. Prices for a hulk start at $10,000, with an operational vehicle going for $25,000. A fully restored vehicle can go for $30,000.

During the late 1950s, the British Army developed a heavy armored car known as the Saladin. Using the lessons learned from WWII-era designed vehicles, the Saladin had six driven wheels to improve its cross-country mobility. Pictured during a British Army parade are both Saladin armored cars and the smaller British Army Ferret scout cars. *Armor magazine*

vanced night-vision devices. The Fox managed to include some of these features in its design, but the cost of the vehicle became so high that the British government couldn't afford to buy as many as it needed.

The Fox was a further development of the late-model Ferret scout cars, except it was built out of aluminum armor rather than steel armor, like the Ferret. The Fox was also much more heavily armed than the Ferret. Equipped with a 30mm Rarden cannon in a two-man turret plus a coaxial 7.62mm machine gun, the Fox could destroy almost any AFV on the battlefield except main battle tanks on their front arc. Its cannon could fire either single, aimed shots or burst up to six rounds. The Fox carried ninety-nine rounds of ammunition. The turret was electrically operated, but could be manually turned if needed.

The Fox was powered by a militarized six-cylinder Jaguar gas engine, giving it a top speed of 65mph and an operating range of almost 250 miles. Drive was transmitted to all

Operated by a crew of three, the Saladin armored car was armed with a 76mm gun. The driver sat in the front hull, and the commander and gunner sat in the turret. Pictured during a training exercise on Cyprus is a Saladin of the British Army. *Armor magazine*

British Fox Armored Scout Car

Looking much like a Ferret in general outline, the Fox armored scout car was designated as a combat vehicle reconnaissance wheeled vehicle by the British Army. It was designed by Daimler, and produced by the Royal Ordnance Factory at Leeds, England. The first-production model came off the assembly line in 1973. After only a few hundred were built, the production line was closed in 1986 by Vickers Defense Systems, who took over the Royal Ordnance Factory.

The Fox was originally designed as the replacement for the Ferret, incorporating all the features the Ferret didn't have, which included better armament and a whole host of ad-

Designed as a replacement for the British Army Ferret scout car was the Fox reconnaissance combat vehicle. It generally followed the same layout as the earlier Ferret scout car, but featured far superior firepower to that of the Ferret. The Fox was fitted with a high-velocity 30mm Rarden gun. The vehicle pictured belonged to the British unit based in former-West Berlin. *Michael Green*

four wheels through a fluid coupling and a five-speed preselective gearbox and transfer box, giving the Fox five speeds both in forward and in reverse. Suspension was independent on all four wheels, with each wheel having an upper and lower wishbone, coil spring, and hydraulic telescopic damper. Steering and brakes were power-assisted, and the four tires were of the run-flat type.

Like the Ferret, the Fox was amphibious only with the help of a collapsible flotation screen, but on the Fox, this collapsible flotation screen was permanently fitted in a stowed position around the top of the hull.

The M114 command and reconnaissance vehicle had a crew of from three to four. Early vehicles were armed (as seen from this overhead photo) with a .50cal machine gun mounted on a rotatable cupola in the center of the vehicle. An M60 7.62mm machine gun could be fired from an open hatch at the rear of the vehicle. *Armor magazine*

The Fox did not share the same sales success as did the earlier Ferret design. The only other countries that bought the Fox were Nigeria, Malawi, Saudi Arabia, and Iran.

With the end of the Cold War and the various disarmament treaties now in effect, at least two Foxes have appeared on the collectors' market. Prices for these vehicle start at $20,000, with a fully restored vehicle going for $45,000. While the Fox has some really neat bells and whistles like night-vision equipment, these devices would be impossible to replace or fix if they broke down. Since there are only a few in collectors' hands, spare parts could be a problem in some cases.

Soviet BRDM-2 Scout Car

The Soviet Army BRDM-2 is a small, fully armored, four-wheel-drive amphibious scout car. Because vehicles of this type tend to belly-out on transverse ridge types of obstacles, the Soviet vehicle designers fitted it with two pairs of small belly wheels under the hull that are chain driven by a power take-off from the main engine and controlled by the driver. Normally, the belly wheels are used only in the most difficult terrain and then only in first gear.

First developed in the early 1960s, the BRDM-2 has seen widespread service with both the Soviet Army and almost forty other countries around the world. It is armed with only a one-man turret mounting a 14.5mm and 7.62mm machine gun, and its thin armor offers protection against small-arms fire only. It is propelled by a single water jet mounted at the rear of the hull. Standard equipment on Soviet military vehicles of this type includes infrared night-vision devices and a tire pressure regulation system that enables the driver to vary the amount of air in the four large wheels. Tire pressure can be lowered on soft ground to provide more ground contact for better mobility and raised on paved roads so that the vehicle can operate at higher speeds.

The BRDM-2 weighs about 7 tons, and is 18ft long, 7ft 3in wide, and 6ft 3in high. It can be operated by two people, but normally has a four-man crew. The turret is the same as the one fitted to the eight-wheeled Soviet BTR60PB APC. The turret has no hatch cover and is manually turned.

The vehicle's 140hp, water-cooled V-8 engine is located in the rear hull. The BRDM-2 can reach a top speed of 50mph and has an operational range of about 310 miles. The suspension system consists of semi-elliptical springs with hydraulic shock absorbers.

The Soviet military adapted the BRDM-2 for a variety of other roles, including a radiological-chemical reconnaissance vehicle with dispensers for placing warning flags around contaminated areas.

Using the chassis of the BRDM-2, the Soviets fitted a surface-to-air launching system with quadruple canisters where the machine gun turret had been mounted. This launcher system was capable of a 360deg traverse and carried a modified version of the SA-7 (Grail) surface-to-air man-portable antiaircraft missile equipped with an infrared homing device and used by Soviet infantry and armored formations.

As an older generation vehicle, the BRDM-2 was being phased out of front-line service prior to the collapse of the USSR, and now that newer generations of Soviet vehicles are on hold, the BRDM-2 and all its variants will continue to see service with the armies of the various new republics for a long time.

Like all former Eastern Bloc AFVs, the BRDM is fairly straight forward and of simple design. It's a fun vehicle to drive with fairly good cross-country mobility. However, if something breaks, finding spares could be a problem. There are also no manuals or spare parts lists for Eastern Bloc equipment, making it very hard to order parts even when you find somebody that may have them.

There are at least five BRDMs in private hands. Prices for an operational vehicle start at $10,000, with a fully restored vehicle going for maybe $18,000.

French Panhard AML

Recently available on the collectors' market are two postwar French light armored cars equipped with a 90mm gun. These vehicles were built by the French firm of Panhard and are part of a series of armored cars with different turrets and weapons known as the AML series. AML stands for Automitrailleuse Légère (light armored car).

The French Army has a long tradition of using lightweight armored cars in the scouting role. Before WWII, the French used many four-wheel-drive armored cars built by Panhard. After France fell in 1940, the Germans began using the French armored cars, so Free French forces were supplied with American tanks and armored cars. After WWII, the French began using a postwar version of their prewar Panhard. These postwar Panhard armored cars, along with a variety of American- and British-built armored cars, were first used in Indochina to suppress the local independence movements. In the 1950s, the former French colony of Algeria also began to struggle for its freedom. Looking for a more modern armored car, the French Army bought a number of British-built Ferrets but found it inadequate for use in Algeria. Looking to its own manufacturers, the French Army requested a four-wheel-drive, lightweight ar-

One of the most unsuccessful scouting vehicles built for the Army during the postwar-era was the M114 command and reconnaissance carrier. First deployed in the early 1960s, originally it was armed only with machine guns. Pictured is an Army M114 in Europe during a 1973 training exercise. *Armor magazine*

First fielded in the Soviet Army in the early 1960s, the BRDM-2 is a fully amphibious scout car armed with a single 14.5mm heavy machine gun in a re-mote-controlled turret. To increase its cross-country mobility, the vehicle has several small belly wheels that can be lowered when needed. *Michael Green*

mored car similar in size and mobility to the British Ferret, but with more firepower. In response, the Panhard Co. in 1960 developed a prototype of a new armored car that became known as the Panhard Model 245 AML.

Armed with a 60mm breech-loaded mortar and a single 12.7mm light machine gun in a two-man turret, the AML went into production in 1961. Since then, more than 4,000 have been built for French and foreign use; South Africa also built, under license, another 1,000 vehicles for its own use. Later versions had a number of different weapon combinations, including 20mm and 30mm high-velocity cannons, antitank missiles, and the 90mm gun (the version now on the collectors' market).

The AML is powered by a Panhard four-cylinder gas engine of 90hp at 4,700rpm. It has a top speed of 62mph and an operational range of about 372 miles.

The AML hull is basically a simple, welded-steel-armor box with the driver in the front, the vehicle's turret in the middle, and the engine in the rear. The driver has a one-piece hatch cover fitted with vision blocks, and the crew can enter or leave through doors on either side of the hull. Its thin armor protects the AML against small-arms fire.

The AML rides on four independently sprung wheels with unpuncturable inner tubes. The wheels are connected to both coil springs and hydro-pneumatic shock absorbers acting on the trailing arms of each wheel mechanism. It is fitted with two hydraulic braking systems, one for the front wheels and one for the rear wheels.

The 90mm gun mounted in the turret of some AML series armored cars fires a fin-stabilized, shaped-charge projectile with a muzzle velocity of 2,450ft per second. Besides the 90mm gun, this same AML version mounts a 7.62mm machine gun to the left of the main gun.

For a very small armored car, the AML armed with the 90mm gun is a very impressive-looking vehicle. Since the vehicle is still

At least one version of the BRDM-2 scout car was modified into an antitank missile-carrying vehicle. The missiles are stored within the hull and are raised into firing position when required. *Greg Stewart*

in widespread service, parts are very expensive. Prices for a hulk start at $5,000, going up to $18,000 for an operational vehicle, to almost $23,000 for a fully restored vehicle.

US M114 Tracked Scouting Vehicle

The former-Army M114 command and reconnaissance carrier is very popular for the collector who wants a fully tracked AFV but does not have the room or money for a tank. Due to its relatively small size—14ft 8in long, 7ft 1in tall, and 7ft 8in wide—the M114 can be easily stored in a backyard shed.

The development of the M114 started in the mid-1950s, when the Army requested a new, fully tracked scouting vehicle. The Army had never been overly fond of wheeled armored cars and after WWII tended to use either unarmored jeeps or light tanks in the scouting role. The M114 was supposed to fall somewhere in between. Being fully tracked, the M114 was intended to have better mobility than a wheeled vehicle. Unlike a tank, the M114 didn't need a large cannon or heavy armor and was equipped with only enough

armor to withstand small arms fire. Since it was not required to engage in combat with enemy forces, only report their positions, the M114 was originally fitted with machine guns only for self-protection.

The first-production M114 entered Army service in 1962. More than 3,701 various models of the M114 were built by Cadillac between 1961 and 1969.

The M114 had thin aluminum armor and a torsion-bar suspension system with four road wheels on either side of the hull, and the drive sprocket at the front and the idler at the rear. A slightly modified version of the M114, known as the M114A1, appeared in 1963.

As time went on, the Army began to think that the trusty old .50cal machine gun mounted on the M114 would not be able to shoot through newer Soviet armored scout cars or APCs. The result was that, in 1968, the M114A1 was now rearmed with a 20mm cannon in a remote-controlled mount. The cannon itself was built under license from the Hispano-Suiza Co. of Switzerland. The commander could select five rates of fire for the

135

20mm cannon, ranging from single shots to five-round bursts at up to 1,000 rounds per minute. This figure is somewhat misleading as the M114 could carry only 100 rounds of 20mm cannon ammunition. Fitted with a 20mm gun, the M114A1 became the M114A2 model.

The M114 was powered by a Chevrolet water-cooled V-8 gas engine of 160hp at 4,600rpm. The engine could push the M114 up to 36mph and gave it an operating range of about 300 miles.

In service use, the mobility of the M114 was a big disappointment to the Army and the troops who had to use it. It was under-powered, not very maneuverable when compared to other similar vehicles, and its tracks tended to come off too easily in hard use.

Although designed to be fully amphibious, when sent to South Vietnam in the early 1960s, the M114 as used by the South Vietnamese Army had great difficulty crossing the numerous rice paddies, streams, and dikes that criss-crossed most of lower South Vietnam. Because of its design, with the front hull beginning at a sharp, protruding angle, every time the vehicle tried to cross a ditch-like obstacle, its front hull would dig into the opposite bank of whatever it was trying to cross. On top of this, the M114 tracks had

The French arms industry has always produced a wide variety of wheeled armored cars mounting a number of different weapons. One of the most heavily armed, light armored cars was the French Panhard AML. *French Army*

trouble achieving traction in the mud. The M114 was withdrawn from South Vietnam and relocated in large numbers with the Army in Europe. It wasn't until the early 1970s that the numerous shortcomings in the M114 finally forced the Army to replace it with the M113 APC.

The generally box-like aluminum shape of the M114 and the M113 leads to some confusion about who built these vehicles and whether the M114 was part of the more popular and well-known M113 family of vehicles. The M114 built by Cadillac and the M113 built by FMC were completely different designs.

When the Army dropped the many thousands of M114s from its inventory in the early 1970s, most became hard targets on Army firing ranges or were scrapped. The Emerson Electronics Co., working under a USAF contract, bought fifty of the surplus M114s and modified them with a variety of electronic equipment to simulate the Soviet Army ZSU-23-4 antiaircraft tank radar systems. These newly-modified M114s are called Tactical Radar Threat Generators and can be found at many USAF training ranges.

The M114 is a good starter vehicle for collectors wanting a fully tracked armored vehicle. The vehicle is easy to work on and parts are readily available at reasonable prices. There are about twenty M114s in private hands. Prices start at $15,000 for a hulk, to $30,000 for an operational vehicle, and up to $40,000 for a fully restored vehicle.

M706 Commando Armored Car

It wasn't until the Vietnam War that the US Army realized that armored cars could still serve a useful purpose. In South Vietnam, Army convoys were suffering heavy losses from enemy ambushes. Military police units assigned to protect the convoys were using makeshift armored trucks and jeeps, but these vehicles proved to be unsatisfactory, so the

Pictured is a French-built Panhard AML armored car belonging to a private collector. Powered by a four-cylinder gas engine, the AML armored car could reach a top speed of 62mph. *Michael Green*

The French-designed-and-built Panhard AML armored car was a four-wheel-drive vehicle armed with a 90mm cannon in a two-man turret. The vehicle pictured is in Israeli Army service. *Israeli Army*

Army quickly began looking around for a more suitable vehicle. It found what it was looking for in a simple, armored car developed by the Cadillac Gage Co. as a private venture in the early 1960s. Known as the V100, this four-wheel-drive vehicle was originally intended as a security vehicle and twelve-person troop transporter for Third World armies that couldn't afford to buy or maintain their own fully tracked vehicles.

The Cadillac Gage Co. had used as many commercial components in the vehicle's design as it could to make it both more affordable and easier to train soldiers on. The V100 was powered by a Chrysler eight-cylinder gas engine mounted in the rear corner of the hull. It weighed about 8 tons, and was 18ft 8in

long, 7ft 5in wide, and about 8ft tall, depending on the turret fitted. It had a top speed of almost 65mph and an operational range of up to 500 miles. The V100 was protected by a well-sloped, steel-armor hull that could deflect most types of small arms fire. With a very short wheelbase and a high 16in ground clearance, the V100 had outstanding cross-country mobility. It was also fully amphibious, its wheels propelling it in the water at about 3mph.

Cadillac Gage referred to its vehicle as the V100 Commando. Designed to be used in a variety of different roles, the V100 could be configured with any number of different weapons. In 1966, the Army began testing the V100, renaming it the M706. After suggesting a few minor changes, the Army decided to buy almost 700 of the M706 for both itself and the South Vietnamese Army.

The M706 was well received by the military police units serving in South Vietnam. The soldiers nicknamed it the "Duck" because of its very pointed front hull. Standard armament for the Army's M706 was a one-man turret armed with two .30cal machine guns. Some American soldiers also mounted a .50cal machine gun on top of the turret, plus numerous M60 7.62mm machine guns on other parts of the vehicle. While the additional machine guns added the extra punch the crews needed to fight their way out of enemy ambushes, it also tended to make the vehicle top-heavy and prone to roll over when turned very sharply.

The biggest problem with the M706 in Vietnam was its weak drivetrain components (brakes, clutch, drive shaft, and rear end), which were 2-1/2 ton Army truck parts and just couldn't handle the strain of the added weight. As experience was gained with the

The M114 command and reconnaissance carrier used by the Army was powered by a Chevrolet V-8 gas engine that gave it a top speed of about 36mph. *Armor magazine*

Owned by a private collector, this M114 has been
stripped, sandblasted, and primed for painting.
Jacques Littlefield

The Cadillac Gage V100 armored car was originally a privately developed venture meant for sale to
Third World countries. Pictured is an M706 hulk belonging to a private collector. The M706 was the
version of the V100 bought by the US Army.
Michael Green

The USAF also used a different version of the Cadillac Gage V100 Commando armored car during the Vietnam War, mainly for airfield protection. It did not have a turret and was open-topped as pictured. *US Army*

M706, Cadillac Gage improved upon the design and later came out with even more impressive vehicles.

The USAF was impressed enough with the Army's M706 that it ordered its own version of the V100 known as the XM706E2. This vehicle, unlike the Army's version, was open-topped and carried a variety of different machine guns. The USAF used sixty of these vehicles in South Vietnam to protect its air bases.

Cadillac Gage sold many V100s to almost a dozen other countries. After the Vietnam War, those M706 vehicles remaining in the Army inventory were phased out of service. The Army did not buy any of the newer vehicles produced by Cadillac Gage.

As with many retired military vehicles, many M706s found their way to firing ranges. Fortunately, seven of them are now in collectors' hands, where at least one has been restored to its former glory.

A really easy vehicle to work on, the M706 is a lot of fun to drive because of its go-almost-anywhere mobility. Parts are available if you look around. Reflecting the high interest in wheeled AFVs, the hulk of an M706 will cost about $15,000, an operational vehicle approximately $35,000, and a fully restored example may go for as much as $55,000.

Pictured in South Vietnamese Army service is this Cadillac Gage armored car known as the V100 Commando. In Army service, the vehicle was known as the XM706. *US Army*

Chapter 6

Miscellaneous Armored Vehicles

German StuG III Armored Assault Vehicle

As early as 1936, the German Army became interested in a special, fully tracked, armored assault vehicle to provide both fire support and antitank protection for its infantry units. The vehicle chosen for this role was the Mk. III medium tank. In its normal configuration, its turret was armed with a 37mm or 50mm gun. To mount a short-barrel 75mm gun and keep the silhouette as low as possible, the gun had to be mounted directly in the hull. While the gun still had some limited traverse, it was generally necessary to move the entire vehicle to aim its gun. This may seem to be a disadvantage, but such a vehicle is easier to hide on a battlefield, and is cheaper and easier to build than a conventional tank. It could also mount a much larger gun than could normally be carried in a turret.

This new armored assault vehicle was known as the Sturmgeschütz III (StuG III for short). Without a turret, the StuG III was only 6ft 5in tall. The normal Mk. III tank with a turret was approximately 8ft high.

In late 1941, Hitler ordered that all future versions of the StuG III have a more powerful gun with antitank capability and better armor protection. In response, the German military mounted a long-barrel 75mm gun in the StuG III. Later models were fitted with machine guns for protection against infantry attacks. Very successful in combat, almost 8,000 StuG III series vehicles were built between 1940 and 1945.

To deal with heavily armored Soviet tanks, the German Army fielded several antitank vehicles during WWII. One of the most successful designs was the StuG III assault gun. By removing the turret of an obsolete Mk. III tank and mounting a long-barreled 75mm cannon in a fixed hull mount, a quick and cheap way was found to provide the German Army with additional antitank firepower in a hurry. *German Army*

Almost 8,000 units of various versions of the German Army StuG III assault gun were built during WWII. The StuG III pictured is on display at the German Army Museum in Munster. *Michael Green*

The vehicle had a four-man crew. It weighed about 20 tons, and was powered by a Maybach twelve-cylinder gas engine, which gave it a top speed of about 25mph and an operational range of 100 miles.

After WWII, most remaining StuG IIIs were scrapped where they stood. France, which had thousands of German AFVs littering its countryside, collected many of them in storage sites, later using them as hard targets on its firing ranges. A few were supplied to former French colonies such as Syria. During its numerous conflicts with Israel over the years, Syria has lost many of its StuG IIIs in combat.

Currently, at least one German StuG III is for sale in the United States. Its owner is asking $150,000. It is visually restored but not operational. Spare parts for foreign AFVs out of production for fifty years can be a problem.

German Hetzer Tank Destroyer

Before WWII, the German Army had given little thought to the development of mobile, fully tracked, antitank vehicles. Its main antitank gun was a 37mm gun towed into action by small trucks. Combat experience quickly taught the Germans that they needed something better to protect their nontank formations from enemy tanks. As a result, in 1939 and 1940, the Germans mounted some of their own antitank guns or captured weapons on obsolete tank chassis. The vehicles tended to be open-topped and poorly protected.

After the invasion of the USSR and General Rommel's desert operations, the German Army desperately demanded tank destroyers. Antitank guns of all types were mounted on anything that could carry their weight, and the Germans began developing better antitank vehicles, known as Panzerjäger or Jadgpanzer.

One of the most successful of these new tank destroyers was known as the Hetzer. Using many components of the obsolete Czech-made LT-35 light tank, more than 2,500 Hetzers were built between 1944 and 1945. The Hetzer was a light, well-protected, turretless vehicle armed with a 75mm gun in a fixed mount in the front hull; the commander, gunner, and loader also rode in the hull. The gun was offset to the right of the hull. The driver sat on the left of the gun. The entire vehicle had to be turned for the gun to be aimed. The armor was 2in thick on the front of the vehicle and 1in thick on the sides of the hull.

The vehicle carried forty-one rounds of 75mm main gun ammunition. Many Hetzers were also fitted with a remote-controlled machine gun mounted on the roof. The Hetzer was powered by a Czech-built Praga AC-2 six-cylinder gas engine. Top speed was about 26mph and operational range was approximately 100 miles.

Many Hetzers were left on the factory production line when WWII ended in Europe. Switzerland bought 158, and the Czech Army retained a large number for years. When Switzerland declared its WWII-era Hetzers obsolete and surplus, at least five were bought for private collections. Reflecting its status as a German AFV from the WWII era, those vehicles available fetch a very high price when placed for sale. A mere hulk will cost at least $50,000, with an operational vehicle bringing over $100,000. A fully restored vehicle could bring as much as $180,000.

US M10 Tank Destroyer

The early success of German armored formations in Poland and France convinced America's military leaders that static (dug-in) defensive positions could not stop mass German tank attacks. To meet this challenge, in 1941, the Army created a new organization known as the Tank Destroyer Branch. By pooling most of its antitank weapons in battalion-sized units, attached to Army divisions, the Army thought that it would have a highly mobile antitank force that could respond to mass German tank attacks anywhere on the battlefield. The motto of this new Branch was "Seek, Strike, and Destroy."

Armed with a 75mm cannon, the Hetzer was adopted in both the Czech and Swiss military service after WWII. After being retired from Swiss military service, a number of these vehicles appeared in private hands. The vehicle pictured belongs to a private collector and is being used during a WWII re-enactment event. *Richard A. Pemberton*

Using the chassis of an obsolete Czech-designed-and-built tank, the German Army developed during WWII a small but effective antitank vehicle known as the Hetzer tank destroyer. Pictured in Germany in 1945 is an American soldier checking out a destroyed Hetzer. *National Archives*

To provide the mobile antitank firepower needed, the Army fielded a number of specially developed tank destroyers, which were supposed to incorporate both outstanding mobility and high firepower. Their job was to engage and destroy enemy tanks, thus allowing American tanks such as the Sherman to concentrate on their primary role of breaking through and destroying enemy rear areas.

While the Tank Destroyer Branch used many different weapons and vehicles to accomplish its mission, its main goal throughout the war was to have put into production a very powerfully armed and highly mobile vehicle as a primary weapon. Unfortunately, wartime demands forced the Tank Destroyer Branch to use the chassis of various model Sherman tanks as an expedient measure.

The first-production fully tracked tank destroyer was the M10. (Earlier tank destroyers had their gun carried either on light trucks or half-tracks.) Mounted on the chassis of the M4A2 Sherman tank, the M10 mounted an obsolete 3in naval gun in an open topped, five-sided turret. The M10 had a five-man crew and carried fifty-four rounds of 3in ammunition. Because it was fitted with lighter armor than that of the standard Sherman, the M10 could reach a top speed of 30mph. Production began in September 1942 and ended in December 1943, with a total of 4,993 M10s built.

Because of the increased demand for additional tank destroyers, Ford Motor Co. was given a contract to build a similar vehicle, but on the chassis of the M4A3 Sherman tank. The

On display at a privately owned military museum in Southern Germany is this Swiss-modified version of the German WWII-era Hetzer tank destroyer. *Richard A. Pemberton*

new vehicle, which carried the same 3in gun as mounted on the M10, was designated the M10A1. A total of 1,413 M10A1s were built through November 1943.

The M10 first saw action in 1943, fighting against Rommel's Afrikakorps in Tunisia. It served throughout WWII from Europe to the Pacific.

The British Army, which received almost 1,700 M10 and M10A1 tank destroyers from the United States during WWII, began converting them in 1944 by replacing the existing 3in guns with their own more powerful 17-pounder gun. In British service, the M10 tank destroyer fitted with the 17-pounder gun was known as the Achilles.

At least one each of the M10A1 and the British-modified Achilles tank destroyer have survived long enough to pass into collectors' hands. Because they are based on the chassis of the Sherman series, engines and many spare parts for the M10 and British Achilles are readily available for a fair price. Other

The US Army also developed a variety of wheeled and tracked tank destroyer vehicles during WWII. One of the best-known and widely used was the M10. Based on the chassis of the M4 Sherman tank, the M10 had a 3in modified naval cannon mounted in an open-topped turret. Pictured are a platoon of American M10s in Germany during WWII. *US Army*

parts unique to the vehicles are a little harder to find.

Despite being much rarer than the typical Sherman, the M10 and British Achilles are about the same price as the Sherman. Hulks start at $20,000, with an operational vehicle selling for around $50,000. A fully restored vehicle might sell for as much as $85,000.

US M56 Scorpion Airborne Self-Propelled Antitank Gun

After WWII, the Army envisioned its airborne and air transportable units playing a very important role in any future armed conflicts. Because the typical tanks of the day weighed more than 25 tons, a very lightweight mobile antitank weapon was needed. As a result, the Army began developing a vehicle known as the M57 Scorpion Airborne Self-Propelled Antitank Gun.

The M56 was armed with a modified 90mm tank gun. Operated by a crew of four, it had no armor protection (to save weight) other than a small gunshield. Made of aluminum, the M56's fully tracked chassis was developed from the M76 Otter amphibious cargo carrier. The engine and transmission of the M56 were located at its front. The 90mm gun was mounted in the center of the vehicle and had very limited traverse. The gun was not stabilized and could not be fired on the move.

Because of the gun's heavy recoil, which tended to move the M56 backwards every time it was fired, the commander had to dismount from the vehicle to see where his gun's rounds hit. The M56 carried twenty-nine rounds of 90mm ammunition in storage racks under the main gun. The vehicle was not fitted with any other armament. The suspension system was of conventional torsion-bar type with hydraulic shock absorbers. There were four rubber-tired road wheels on each side of the hull. The drive sprocket was at the front and the idler was at the rear. The tracks were of an unusual, continuous rubber and fabric construction with steel bars permanently embedded into the fabric for better traction. The M56 was 15ft long and 8ft 6in wide. With its gunshield fitted, the vehicle was 6ft 9in tall.

After WWII, the only true tank destroyer built for the Army was the M56 Scorpion. Armed with a 90mm gun on basically an unarmored tracked chassis, the lightweight Scorpion was designed for airborne units. *US Army*

Owned by a private collector, this M56 Scorpion is in running condition but is still missing a number of original parts. *Michael Green*

Power was provided by a Continental six-cylinder, air-cooled gas engine. Top speed was about 30mph with an operational range of about 140 miles.

The M56 first came off the Cadillac production line in 1953. A total of 226 M56 vehicles were built before production ended in May 1959.

A handful of M56s saw service for a brief period during the Vietnam War. However, their lack of crew protection caused them to be replaced by newer vehicles, such as the M113 APC and the M551 Sheridan armored reconnaissance airborne assault vehicle. The last M56 disappeared from the Army inventory sometime in the mid-1960s.

Both Morocco and Spain were supplied with M56s sometime in the late 1960s, but due to a lack of spare parts, both countries' military units no longer use the vehicle.

At least six M56s, minus their original 90mm guns, have appeared in collectors' hands. At least one collector has fitted a standard 90mm tank gun on his M56 chassis to give it the appearance of a production vehicle.

Spare parts for the M56 are fairly hard to find. The vehicle itself is both fast and maneu-verable due to its lack of armor. Prices range from $15,000 for a hulk, to $30,000 for an operational vehicle, up to $60,000 for a fully restored vehicle.

US M50 Ontos Light Armored Antitank Vehicle

In the early 1950s, the Army began looking at the development of a lightweight, fully tracked, armored antitank vehicle to replace its unarmored jeeps in antitank units. In response to the Army's interest, the Allis-Chalmers Manufacturing Co. built a new tracked vehicle to fit the Army's needs. In the meantime, unfortunately, the Army had decided it couldn't afford the new vehicle and decided to stick with its jeep-mounted antitank units.

Fortunately for the Allis-Chalmers Co., the USMC was looking for a new antitank vehicle to replace its fleet of aging Sherman tanks. As a result, in 1955 the M50 entered production for the USMC. A total of 684 vehicles were built. The official US military name for the M50 was the Ontos. The name Ontos meant the "Thing" in Greek.

What made this nickname so appropriate for the M50 was its appearance. Instead of mounting a standard tank gun, the M50 was armed with six recoilless rifles attached to a pivoting fixture mounted on the roof. The rifles would all elevate or turn together, but they could be fired singly or all at the same time. This gave the M50 a massive amount of firepower for such a small vehicle (about 7 tons). The M50 was about 12ft 6in long, 9ft 6in wide, and about 7ft tall.

The drawback to this firepower was that recoilless rifles produce a very large backblast every time they are fired. For this reason, the M50's recoilless rifles had to be mounted on the outside of the hull. The large backblast from the recoilless rifles also attracted enemy attention to the vehicle's location (a serious problem in combat).

The crew of the M50 consisted of a driver, loader, and vehicle commander. The vehicle was powered by a Chrysler eight-cylinder gas engine, which gave it a top speed of about 30mph. Operational range was approximately 150 miles. Armor protection was less than 1/4in thick.

Besides the six short-range 106mm recoilless rifles, the M50 was armed with a single .30cal machine gun operated by the commander.

The M50 first saw combat in 1965, when it was used by the USMC in the invasion of the Dominican Republic. The M50s saw their most extensive combat action during the Viet-

First placed into service in 1953, the M56 Scorpion armed with a 90mm gun saw limited action during the Vietnam War. Due to its open-topped design, it was fairly quickly withdrawn from service. The M56 Scorpion pictured is being used in action during the Vietnam War in July 1966. *US Army*

nam War. However, the vehicle was not well suited to a guerrilla war. Its thin armor made it very susceptible to Vietcong mines. This, and the need to reload the vehicle's weapons from outside made its crew very vulnerable to Vietcong snipers.

By 1970, the USMC considered tanks a better choice than the M50. All the M50s in the USMC inventory were scrapped. Most of them found their way to various firing ranges, but a few M50s, in various stages of restoration, have appeared in collectors' hands. As of yet, only one collector has mounted nonoperational recoilless rifles on his vehicle to restore it to its original appearance. The M50 is a great running little tracked vehicle; it's fairly simple to maintain. Parts are out there if you look around. Prices for a hulk start at $10,000, with an operational vehicle going for $20,000. A fully restored vehicle would sell anywhere from $40,000 to $45,000.

Originally designed for the Army, the M50 Ontos was instead adopted into USMC service. The small vehicle was armed with six 106mm recoilless rifles mounted outside the hull. Pictured is a head-on shot of a USMC M50 Ontos at a training base. *USMC*

Like many obsolete AFVs, this M50 Ontos, minus its weapons, is now a target on a firing range. *USAF*

US M19 Antiaircraft Vehicle

During WWII, the US Army tested many different antiaircraft weapons fitted to a wide variety of wheeled half-track and fully tracked vehicles. The only such vehicles to make it into American use during the war were based on half-tracks.

Because of the half-tracks' very poor cross-country mobility, the Army's Antiaircraft Branch wanted to mount its weapons on a converted M5A1 light tank hull. However, as production of this vehicle was soon to end in favor of the M24 light tank, the Army decided to mount twin 40mm antiaircraft guns on the hull of the M24. This new vehicle became known as the M19.

To make room for the twin 40mm gun mount and its crew of four men, the M24 hull was modified by moving the vehicle's engine and transmission to the front of the hull. At the rear of the hull was an open-topped, power-operated, rotating mount. The twin 40mm gun mount had a 360deg traverse and could be raised to an elevation of 85deg. The gun-operating crew was protected by a thinly armored shield only. In addition to their anti-aircraft role, the M19 guns could be used as ground support. The M19 was produced too late to see action during WWII, but it was used during the Korean War. As there was little threat to United Nations ground units from the North Korean or Chinese Air Force, the M19 was used mostly as a fast-firing armored assault gun to assist infantry units.

Almost 300 M19s were built by both Cadillac and the Massey-Harris Co. Because it was based on the gas-powered hull and suspension system of the M24 light tank, it shared the same short operating range of all AFVs of its period.

Based on the chassis of an Army M24 light tank was the M19 self-propelled twin 40mm armed anti-aircraft vehicle. First built in 1945, it was too late to see combat in WWII, but it did see extensive service during the Korean War. *US Army*

As the M19 was replaced by newer vehicles, most were sent to firing ranges. At least three M19s have passed into collectors' hands. Being based on the chassis of the M24 light tank means that both engines and many parts are available for the M19. The vehicle is both faster and has better cross-country mobility than the standard M24 light tank since it is not carrying around an armored turret. Unfortunately, some items of the M19 are almost impossible to find, like the twin 40mm barrels. Some collectors have been forced to make their own dummy barrels.

Prices for a M19 hulk start at $20,000, with an operational model selling for $35,000, and a fully restored model selling for $50,000.

US M42 Duster Antiaircraft Vehicle

To replace the M19 antiaircraft vehicle based on the chassis of the M24 light tank, the US Army began work in early 1951 on the development of a new antiaircraft vehicle that became known as the M42 Duster. The M42 was based on the chassis of the Army's new M41 light tank. Production of the M42 started in 1952 by Cadillac and ended in 1957, with about 3,700 vehicles being built. A few vehicles were also built by ACF Industries, Inc.

The M42 used a modified version of the twin 40mm gun mount found on the earlier M19. Unlike the M19, the gun mount of the M42 was in the center of the hull. The other four crewmen sat in the turret and operated the twin 40mm antiaircraft guns. Like the M19 gun mount, the M42 gun mount had a 360deg traverse and could be turned by a power-operated system, 40deg per second. Both the M19 and M42 had a manually operated backup system for turning the guns if the power system was lost. Like the M19, the M42 gun crew had no protection other than a thinly armored gunshield.

The 40mm guns, known as Bofors, could be fired in single rounds or fully automatic. Their maximum rate of fire was about 120 rounds per minute, per barrel. The M42 could carry about 480 rounds of ammunition. Some of the rounds were carried in the turret; others were stored in lockers on either side of the hull. All ammunition was mounted in five-round clips. The M42 was also fitted with a .30cal or 7.62cal M60 machine gun.

Because the M42 was never fitted with a radar system, it could not operate at night or in poor weather conditions.

The M42 was supplied to a number of friendly governments, including West Germany, Japan, Jordan, Austria, and Lebanon.

In service with the Army, the M42 saw its first combat action during the Vietnam War. Like the M19 during the Korean War, the M42 had no enemy aircraft to engage, and it was used primarily as a fire-support vehicle. In addition to being used as base security guards, M42s were also used in the convoy escorting business. American soldiers involved in enemy ambushes appreciated their heavy firepower.

By the late 1970s, the M42 was showing its age and was slowly phased out of regular Army service. The last M42s saw service in Army National Guard units up until a few years ago.

Up to half-a-dozen or more of the M42s are now in collectors' hands. The hardest part of restoring the M42 is trying to find the twin

The twin 40mm guns mounted in the M19 self-propelled antiaircraft vehicle were among the most widely used weapons in the American air defense from WWII through the 1960s. Pictured in South Korea in 1954 is this Army M19 positioned in a dug-in emplacement overlooking a Korean city. Notice the spare 40mm gun barrels on the left of the vehicle. *US Army*

As the M24 light tank was replaced in Army service by the M41 light tank, the Army began to develop a new antiaircraft vehicle based on the chassis of the M41 light tank. Mounting the same twin 40mm guns as found on the earlier M19, the new vehicle was known as the M42 Duster. The M42 was widely used in the ground-support role during the Vietnam War. *US Army*

40mm gun barrels. Most were removed by the American military when the vehicles were scrapped.

M42 engines and many parts are not hard to find nor are they expensive. Prices for the M42 range from $20,000 for a hulk, to $35,000 for an operational vehicle, and up to $50,000 for a fully restored vehicle.

US M7 Self-Propelled Artillery

In late 1941, Maj. Gen. Jacob L. Devers, Chief of the Army Armored Forces and a former artilleryman, recommended that the Army take its standard towed 105mm field howitzer and mount it on the chassis of an M3 medium tank. He hoped to see produced a self-propelled artillery gun that could keep up with fast-moving armored formations.

After testing at Aberdeen Proving Grounds and Fort Knox, the Army approved production. The vehicle was standardized in April 1942 as the M7. British soldiers who used it in North Africa nicknamed the M7 the "Priest" because they thought its armor-protected, .50cal antiaircraft mount on the right front hull resembled a church pulpit.

The M7 was a very simple vehicle with a 105mm field howitzer mounted in a box-like armored superstructure. The gun was serviced by a crew of five and could fire to a range of about 7 miles.

Based on the chassis of the Army's M3 and M4 medium tank was the M7 series of 105mm self-propelled guns. First fielded in 1943, the M7 proved to be a most effective weapon during WWII. Belong-ing to a private collector, this late-model M7 is being restored to operational condition by its owner. *Michael Green*

A total of 3,490 M7 self-propelled artillery vehicles were built on the chassis of the M3 medium tank. A further 826 vehicles known as M7B1 and based on the chassis of the M4A3 Sherman tank were built by the Pressed Steel Car Co. during WWII. Both vehicles were very similar in appearance. The only major difference was the engines. Both the M7 and M7B1 remained in the Army inventory until after the Korean War. A large number were later supplied to other countries as military aid. At least a dozen M7 and M7A1s have survived into collectors' hands.

Based on the chassis of both the M3 and M4 medium tanks, the M7 is easy to maintain because engines and many other parts are readily available. Because they don't have a turret, M7s make an excellent vehicle to give rides in. The 105mm gun is also a neat display feature for a collector. Prices for hulks start at $25,000 and go up to $60,000 for an operational vehicle. A fully restored vehicle can cost $75,000.

British Sexton Self-Propelled Gun/Howitzer

The British military was so impressed with the M7 that it decided to copy the concept. Using a Canadian-built version of the M4A1 Sherman known as the Grizzly 1, the British had Canadian manufacturers mount their well-known 25-pounder gun/howitzer in a thin, open-topped superstructure on top of the Canadian tank chassis. The gun/howitzer was located at the front of the rear hull, with the transmission at the front.

The 25-pounder gun/howitzer (approximately 88mm) was originally developed by

Replaced in Army service by newer vehicles after the Korean War, the M7 continued to serve in foreign armies for many decades. As a result, several have survived and passed into collectors' hands.

Pictured is an M7 owned by a private collector, which has been sitting in an open field for too long. *Jacques Littlefield*

the British in 1935. Unlike the American 105mm howitzer mounted in the M7, the British weapon was fitted with a double-baffle muzzle brake and had both direct and indirect firing ability. During the early North African battles between the Germans and the British, the 25-pounder gun/howitzer was successfully used as an antitank gun.

This combination of a British-designed-and-built gun/howitzer mated to the Canadian-built tank was officially known as the 25-pounder Self-Propelled Tracked Sexton. Most people just called it the Sexton for short.

Development of the Sexton had begun in late 1942. Production started in 1943, and about 2,000 were built before the war ended in 1945. Used by the British Army until the 1950s, the Sexton was also supplied to India, South Africa, and Portugal; Portugal sold its entire fleet of Sextons to an American dealer.

Approximately twenty-five were brought into the United States in 1982. Currently, an operational Sexton can be bought for as little as $10,000. A fully restored model could cost $25,000.

Soviet Scud A Transporters

Employed in Soviet military service beginning in the mid-1950s was a large surface-to-surface ballistic missile carried on a heavily modified tank chassis. Known by its NATO code name of "SCUD," the American public quickly became aware of the missile when it posed a threat to both American and Allied forces during Operation Desert Storm. Supplied by the USSR to Iraq beginning in the 1970s, the SCUD missile was itself copied by the Soviets from captured German V-2 rockets shortly after WWII.

One of the most unusual military vehicles in private hands is the early version of the Soviet SCUD missile-launcher unit based on a Soviet heavy tank from the WWII-era. The rocket itself was copied by the Soviets from captured German V-2 rockets. The vehicles pictured are taking part in an Eastern European military parade sometime in the early 1960s. *Chris Foss*

When first built, the Soviet military mounted the 40ft long SCUD missile and its launcher unit on the chassis of a WWII-era heavy tank, known as the JS-III. With its turret removed, the Soviets built up an unarmored cabin at the front of the vehicle to house the driver and the missile-launching crew. The SCUD missile was launched vertically and was raised into position by large hydraulic jacks which cradled the missile in an open-ladder framework platform. The SCUD missile had a maximum range of about 180 miles. The Iraqi version of the SCUD missile could fly almost 400 miles.

After being fired, the SCUD A transporter vehicle is immediately driven to a new location to avoid an enemy counterattack and then reloaded with another missile from a support vehicle.

Beginning in the early 1960s, the Soviets replaced the fully tracked JS III chassis with a large, unarmored eight-wheel cross-country truck chassis. This version of the SCUD missile and its launcher/transport vehicle is what the Iraqi military used during Operation Desert Storm.

In early 1991, a British dealer managed to acquire an early model of the SCUD missile-launcher vehicle mounted on the JS III tank chassis. Fitted with a dummy missile, the SCUD A transporter presents a one-of-a-kind military vehicle, wherever it may be displayed. The price of this type of AFV is hard to determine. Only a very specialized collector could possibly have the space or money to care for such a vehicle.

US M32 Series Tank-Recovery Vehicles

In the years before WWII, the Army used large, wheeled wrecker trucks (tow trucks) to recover disabled or stuck light tanks. As bigger and heavier tanks such as the Sherman entered the inventory, the Army quickly found that the best way to recover a damaged tank was by using another tank. At first, the Army used the chassis of the M3 medium tank as the basis for a tank-recovery vehicle, stripping the M3 of its guns and adding a winch and jib crane with an A-frame support mounted to it. As the supply of M3 medium tanks became shorter, the Army decided to use the chassis of various models of the Sherman tank as the basis of a new and improved tank-recovery vehicle. Each model had a different designation: The M4 became the M32 tank-recovery vehicle; the M4A1, the M32B1;

Patterned after the American-designed-and-built M7 series of self-propelled howitzers was the British version, known as the Sexton. Built on the chassis of a Canadian-built tank known as the Ram, the Sexton mounted a British 25-pounder artillery cannon. In wide use during and after WWII, several of these vehicles have passed into collectors' hands. *British Army*

To help recover broken down or damaged tanks, the Army developed during WWII an entire series of armored, fully tracked, recovery vehicles based on the chassis of various M4 Sherman tanks. Pictured is one example of a Sherman-based armored recovery vehicle. *US Army*

the M4A2, the M32B2; the M4A3, the M32B3; and the M4A4, the M32B4.

All of the Sherman-based M32 series of tank-recovery vehicles were equipped with a fixed turret made out of steel plates. Part of their standard recovery equipment was a 60,000lb-capacity winch and a movable crane-type boom with a lifting capacity of 30,000lb. Some Sherman-based tank-recovery vehicles featured an 81mm mortar mounted on the front of the hull to fire smoke shells to help hide the recovery of vehicles when under enemy fire.

As the Sherman was improved, so were the tank-recovery vehicles of the M32 series. Later models featured the wider tracks of the horizontal volute-spring suspension system, as well as all the other internal changes found in second-generation Sherman tanks.

By the Korean War, the Army had developed a new tank-recovery vehicle based on an M4A3 Sherman chassis. Known as the M74, this vehicle had a 90,000lb-capacity winch, a hydraulically operated crane-type boom, and, unlike the earlier M32 series, a dozer blade at the front of the vehicle to aid in recovery operations.

For the collector who likes his tanks large and likes to drive them, a tank recovery vehicle is a must. Even for nonrunning hulks, there is always a need to be able to move them at different times. Without such a vehicle, it would be very difficult to enter into collecting the larger and more interesting AFVs.

At least five M32 series tank-recovery vehicles are now in private hands. Prices for an M32 series vehicle start at $15,000 for a hulk, reach $25,000 for an operational vehicle, and approach $40,000 for a fully restored vehicle.

Index